Great Dictations

Books by Judy DeFilippo and Catherine Sadow:

Basic Dictations • text and CD
Launched Beginner

Great Dictations • text and CD
High Beginner to Low Intermediate

Interactive Dictations • text and CD
Low Intermediate to Intermediate

Dictations for Discussion • text and 2 CDs
Intermediate to Advanced

Great Dictations

A Listening/Speaking Text for High Beginner and Low Intermediate ESL Students

Second Edition

Catherine Sadow
Judy DeFilippo

PRO LINGUA LEARNING

Pro Lingua Learning
PO Box 4467
Rockville, MD 20849 USA
Office: 301-424-8900
Orders: 800-888-4741
Email: info@ProLinguaLearning.com
Web: www.ProLinguaLearning.com

*At **Pro Lingua***
our objective is to foster an approach
to learning and teaching that we call
***interplay,** the **inter**action of language*
learners and teachers with their materials,
with the language and culture,
and with each other in active,
creative, and productive
play.

ISBN 13: 978-0-86647-364-4

Great Dictations was designed by Arthur A. Burrows. It was set in Palatino, the most widely used, and pirated, face of the twentieth century, which was designed by Hermann Zapf in 1948 in Frankfurt. Although modern, it is based on Renaissance designs typical of the Palatinate area in Germany.

The photographs illustrating this book are from Dreamstime.com Agency, except as noted: p. 1 Zeus © Georgios Kollidas, Olympia © Dr. Le Thanh Hung, p. 6 © Ukrphoto, p. 9 © Bruce Macqueen, p. 12 © Olesya Nosova, p. 21 © Sparkia, p. 22 © Toby Armstrong/web, p 25 © Mikosha Natalia Gudyma, p. 27 © Kuco, p. 29 © Danomyte, p. 31 © Rockpig Zhang Liwei, p. 35 © Jacetan, p. 37 © Jennifer Hogan, p. 39 © Cafebeanz Company, p. 41 © Ken Hurst, p. 44 © Daniel Wiedemann, p. 48 © Chantal Ringuette, p. 51 © Jperagine, p. 52 © Monkey Business Images,, p. 53 © John Takai, p. 55 © William Howell, p. 60 © Misty Pfeil, p. 65 © Radu Razvan, p 72 © left Sjhuls and right Annems, p. 74 © Rosa Parks Museum in Montgomery, Alabama, p. 79 © Christophe Rolland, p. 81 © Janos Sison, p. 83 © Forestpath, p. 87 © Kalin Eftimov, p. 91 © Jamie Roach, p. 93 © Connie Larsen, p. 96 © Alain, p. 98 © Jerome Sadow, p. 102 © Maja Schon, p. 105 © Joseph Cortes, p. 106 Robert Florian, p. 108 © Imagecollect, p. 111 © Cafebeanz Company, p. 115 © John "Winter" Smith selfie from Facebook with permission, p. 124 © Mattyc1965, p 129 © Conde. The cover photo of the Great Lake Lighthouse in Duluth, Minnesota (taken on: July 04th, 2008 at Sunrise) is © Geoffrey Kuchera: Dreamstime.

Contents

Dictogloss and Partial Dictations ✣ 22

Pair Dictations ❋ 40

❀ *Acknowledgements* ❀

The authors based many of their activities on concepts introduced by P. Davis and M. Rinvolucri, who co-authored *Dictation, New Methods, New Possibilities*, Cambridge University Press.

The authors are grateful to the authors and publishers whose facts and figures are cited:

The Boston Globe:
"American Families" by Patricia Wen
"Better Late Than Never to Achieve Goals" by Matt Viser

The New York Post:
"The Return of the Melting Pot" by Linda Chavez

The New York Times:
"Japan Seeking to Trim Waists" by Norimitsu Onishi
"Marry Me at 8 on the 8th, OK?" by Jennifer Lee

Various Internet Sources

Oprah's School in South Africa
Valentine's Day
Council on Contemporary Families & Researchers
National Virtual Translation Center: Charts on World Languages
Coffee, Coffee, and More Coffee
Alia Sabur – College Professor at 19
Japan 101 – Overworked
Wikipedia – Wild Turkeys, Family Names
Essortment.com – Shopaholics
Pandas International – Giant Pandas
Ten Things That Will Disappear in Our Lifetime
International Baseball

The authors wish to thank the following teachers who field-tested the text and gave valuable feedback:

Linda Hasenfus, EF – Education First, Brighton, MA
The Faculty at Showa Boston

Introduction

Great Dictations is a high beginner/low intermediate–level text that is intended to improve the listening and speaking skills of ESL students. Reading and writing skills are also reinforced, along with attention to vocabulary and grammar. This text provides a wide variety of dictation topics, including provocative news items and information from the internet.

The units are designed to stand alone so that teachers can pick and choose which dictations meet the needs, interests, and levels of their students. Each unit begins with a short **introduction** that provides a background and context for the dictation. The introduction is followed by a short list of **vocabulary** items whose meanings are central to the dictation. The list also provides a chance to hear the teacher pronounce these important vocabulary items. The central focus of the unit is a **dictation** activity. In some chapters there is an additional listening activity. Each dictation/listening is followed by a **discussion** section. The discussions can take place in pairs or small groups. With some units, the teacher may want to discuss the issues with the whole class. The units end with a **follow-up** activity which is intended to explore the topic further – often by having students speak with native speakers. The follow-up also provides additional language skill practice, especially writing practice.

Most units are two or three pages long. Some units will take less time than others, so a shorter unit or part of a unit can be done as a fill-in. The dictations usually take about 30 minutes. The discussions take from 20 to 30 minutes. Some follow-up activities are done in class and some are done out of class to be continued during the next class meeting. Longer units with in-class follow-up activities will take 30 to 50 minutes.

The **complete texts** of the dictations begin on page 93. These full texts can be read to the students, or a student can read them to the class. They are also available on a CD.

❀ Different Types of Dictations ❀

Dictation has been presented in many forms through the years in reading, listening, grammar, and writing classes. It is also used as an assessment procedure. This text, however, does not deal with scoring or analyzing student work. The dictations are meant to be a challenging springboard to discussion and writing by which the students are encouraged to use the language they have just encountered in the dictation.

This text includes four forms of dictation: **partial, pair, dictogloss,** and **prediction.**

1. Partial (sometimes known as *cloze*)

Most of the dictations in this text are partial dictations where words, phrases, or chunks of language have been deleted, and students are required to listen and write down the missing words. All the dictations should be discussed upon completion. Pair work is encouraged, and spelling can be corrected.

2. Pair (sometimes known as mutual)

This dictation requires students to work in pairs to combine two partial texts into one continuous piece. One student (Student A) has a gapped copy of the dictation, and the other student (Student B) has a differently gapped copy. Each student has half of the text. They should not look at each other's sheets. Student A dictates and Student B writes, then B dictates and A writes, back and forth, and so on until the story is complete. The first one the students do should be modeled first.

3. Dictogloss

In this kind of dictation, the focus is on getting the gist or main idea of a sentence or short paragraph.

There are many variations of the dictogloss technique. In the directions for the sentence-level dictogloss, students are told that they will hear a sentence **only once**, after which they are to jot down the words they can recall and try to reconstruct the sentence in writing as accurately as they can. The first time this is done, the teacher will probably have to allow the students a second reading until they discover that they need to pay attention the first time around. This is especially true for high beginner/low intermediate–level students. As the students work at rebuilding the sentences, they can work in pairs or groups of three or four. Some teachers like to have students write their sentences on the board for all to see and discuss.

4. Prediction

Prediction lessons come in two parts. The first part focuses more on reading skills and grammar. The students can work individually or in pairs, reading the passage and predicting (or guessing) what should be in each blank space. Any logical or grammatically correct word or phrase can be accepted. The second part requires the students to listen to the same passage and see if their guesses were correct, or similar.

❀ Tips for Teachers ❀

1. When reading the full dictations, try to speak naturally, at normal speed, keeping the features of the spoken language. If you are reading the full text at normal speed and you know the exercise will be fairly easy for your students, give the word, phrase, or chunk of language only once. Try to start with a pace that is comfortable for your students, and then make them work a bit at understanding. If you think the text will be difficult for your students, repeat two, possibly three times. When field testing our material, several teachers said they thought the material looked quite difficult for their students, but they were surprised how well their students did. It's up to you to decide what works best. If you have to repeat more than three times, the text is too difficult for your students.

2. The students may want to check the spelling of a word or words as you are giving the dictation. It's best to tell them to wait until the end of the activity.

3. For numbers, have the students write numerals, rather than the word (15, instead of fifteen), except for single-digit numbers (1–9). They should also use dollar ($) and percentage (%) symbols rather than writing out the words.

4. One key to making the dictation a positive experience is to have students correct their own work. When the dictation is completed, the students in pairs check with each other on what they've heard, while you walk around helping and clarifying. This in itself allows for a great deal of discussion. After they have self-corrected, they can turn to the full dictation texts for confirmation. You can then go over the dictation with the class and discuss whatever vocabulary or concepts they don't understand.

5. Rather than read the full dictations, you may find it helpful to copy the page you're dictating and fill in the blanks ahead of time. This is helpful when giving your students feedback. It's easier when you're working from the same page as your students. Here is an example from "Trivia Contest."

   1. Where can __you__ __buy__ a Whopper Junior?
   2. Who ____wrote____ *Romeo and Juliet*?

6. There is no single pattern that was followed when choosing words or phrases to be deleted. Sometimes the deletions focus on idioms, sometimes on numbers, sometimes grammar, sometimes vocabulary.

7. ***Great Dictations*** also works well for substitute teachers, since a minimum amount of preparation is needed.

8. You and your students can also create dictations from local newspapers, the internet, or any other source. This way you can choose a timely topic and easily adapt it to the level of your students.

9. Discussions can be in pairs, small groups, or the entire class. In some units there are two discussions. They can be done in any order. To save time, one can be eliminated.

❀ Pronunciation ❀

When introducing the vocabulary, you may want to ask students to repeat some of the words or phrases after you introduce them. Students often know the meaning of words but are afraid to use them because they don't know what they sound like. They'll probably need to use some of the words in the discussion that follows the dictation and will feel freer to use them if they have already said them aloud.

❀ Using the CD ❀

On the CD, each dictation text is on a separate track. The CD track numbers are given in the table of contents, beneath the titles of the gapped texts, and next to the page numbers of the full dictation texts.

Although it is not necessary to have and use the accompanying CD, many teachers find that having the CD provides greater flexibility in using the material. It can be used in several ways:

1. Play the track once through without stopping, before reading the dictation to the students. This will introduce the topic and give the students a head start toward comprehending the dictation when it is read to them.

2. To give the students a chance to hear a different voice, have the students take the dictation from the CD. Although more challenging, this can help students prepare for standardized listening tests. You can use the pause button; that will allow the students time to fill in the blanks.

3. Play the CD **after** the students have taken the dictation and checked their answers. This can help students improve and become more confident in listening comprehension.

❀ Using a Listening Laboratory ❀

Almost any dictation that is done in class can also be done in the listening lab. However, there are additional things that can be done in the lab that cannot be done in a classroom.

1. Read a short and easy partial dictation in the lab. The dictation can be from this text or something you have devised on your own. Then have the students record what they have written. You can collect both, and then on the student CD, give them some feedback on their pronunciation. If they can do this successfully, next time make the dictation a little longer.

2. Dictate a problem. An example might be a "Dear Abby" letter that you have turned into a dictation (or try one of the Abby-type letters in this text). After each student has done the dictation, they record the solution to the problem. You should listen and respond to the solution, or the students can move from station to station to listen to their fellow students and make comments of agreement or disagreement. By preparing short, easy-to-understand dictations first, you can also use this technique to introduce other survival or cultural topics that you think will be of particular interest to your students.

❀ About the Full Dictation Texts ❀

The complete texts for the dictations begin on page 93. You can do the dictations by reading these full texts. The missing words are in bold and underlined.

To
the two Jerrys

The Olympic Games

full text on page 93 (cd track 1)

Introduction ❁

The Olympic Games are the world's most important international sports competition. There are winter games and summer games every four years in a different country. Will the Olympics come to your country in the future?

Vocabulary, Pronunciation ❁

1. **an athlete**: a person who plays sports well
2. **an event**: a happening

Zeus at Olympia, Greece

Dictation ❁

Listen and write the word or words you hear in the blank spaces. Check your answers with a partner.

1. The very first Olympic Games ______________ _____ Greece almost 3,000 years ago. In those early years there were simple foot races ________ horse races. ________ ___________ honored the god Zeus and __________ ________ in the town of Olympia. These games _______________ for 600 __________ and then ____________ because people stopped believing in ________ ________.

2. The modern games __________ again in 1896 in Athens, Greece, with 250 athletes from _______countries. Women entered the Olympics ____ ___________ ____________. In the 2004 Summer Olympics in Athens, there were 11,000 athletes from 202 _________________ _________________________.

3. The Olympic flag has _________ ____________. The colors on the rings are ______, _________, blue, green, yellow, and black ________________each country in the Olympics has at least one of these colors in its national______________. What colors _______ ______ your country's flag?

Discussion

Here is a list of past and present venues for the Modern Games.

Summer		**Winter**	
1924	Paris, France	1952	Oslo, Norway
1968	Mexico City, Mexico	1984	Sarajevo, Bosnia and Herzogovina
1980	Moscow, Russia	1988	Calgary, Canada
1988	Seoul, South Korea	1998	Nagano, Japan
2008	Beijing, China	2010	Vancouver, Canada
2012	London, Great Britain	2014	Sochi, Russia
2016	Rio de Janeiro, Brazil	2018	Pyeongchang, South Korea
2020	Tokyo, Japan	2022	____________________

Decide where you want to see the Summer and Winter Olympic Games held in 2024, 2026, 2028, and 2030. Work with a partner.

Summer 2024 ____________________ Winter 2026 ____________________

Summer 2028 ____________________ Winter 2030 ____________________

Class Contest

Work in groups of two or three and make two lists: (1) Summer Olympics and (2) Winter Olympics. Use the list below and write the sport that goes in each category. You can add more if you want! The group with the most correct sports wins the contest.

boxing	tennis	downhill skiing
figure skating	soccer	weightlifting
snowboarding	tae kwon do	volleyball
speed skating	ice hockey	bobsledding
swimming	bicycling	cross country skiing

Discussion

Younger athletes can compete in the Youth Olympic Games. These games are for athletes between ages 14 and 18. With a partner, answer these questions.

1. What sports do you think these young athletes will be good in?
2. Why did the Olympic Committee decide to do this?
3. Education and culture will be a part of these events. Why is this important?

Follow-up activities

1. *Write or tell the class about a sport you are interested in. Do you play it or watch it? Are you are on a team? Explain why you like it.*

2. *Find out about the "Special Olympics."*
   If possible, check this website: SpecialOlympics.org/world_games.aspx

About Lying

full text on page 94 (cd track 2)

Introduction ❁

Our parents and teachers tell us that lying is bad, and that we should always tell the truth. They punish us when we lie. Recently, however, some psychologists have done a lot of research on lying, and they have a different view. What do you think?

Vocabulary, Pronunciation ❁

1. **ashamed**: feeling guilty and sad
2. **to protect**: to defend against harm or loss
3. **a resumé**: a written history of your education and work experience
4. **a politician**: a person who runs for a government office, such as a mayor or president

Dictation ❁ **Part 1.** *Write the words you hear in the blank spaces. If you agree with the statement, write (A) next to the number. If you disagree, write (D). Then compare and discuss your answers with a partner and the class.*

___ 1. Some people lie because __________ _______ ashamed to tell the truth.

___ 2. __________________we lie to protect other people.

___ 3. Politicians lie _____ ____________.

___ 4. _________ lie more than _______________.

Dictation ❁ **Part 2.** *Listen and write the words you hear.*
Decide whether the following lies are serious (S) or not-so-serious (NSS).

___ 1. You ______________ _____ your homework because you went ____ ___ ____________ the night before. To your teacher you say, "____ ________ _______."

___ 2. Bob and his ______________, Mary, are going to get married ________ ________, but he went out with another girl last Saturday. When Mary ________ ______ where he was on Saturday, Bob said, "I was ______ _______ ______________."

___ 3. Your _______________ just had a baby boy. When you first see the baby, ______ ____________ he's ugly, but you look at your sister and say, "______ cute!"

___ 4. Susan wrote on her resumé that she graduated ____________ Harvard University. She took _______ _______________ there.

Discussion ❁ *Talk about these situations with a partner. Then share your ideas with the class.*

1. Would you say this to ___________? Why or why not?
   a. your friend: "Those pants make you look fat."
   b. your five-year-old niece: "No, Virginia, there is no Santa Claus."
   c. your friend: "I don't like your new haircut."

2. Lying in my culture is ____________.
   a. never acceptable
   b. acceptable in some situations
   c. acceptable in adults, not children
   d. other: ________________________________

3. Here are some quotes about lying. Do you agree or disagree?
   a. "Telling the truth is not about making you feel better. Sometimes it is as painful to tell the truth as it is to hear it."
   b. "We don't have to tell the truth if it hurts someone's feelings."
   c. "If you always tell the truth you never have to remember which lies you told."

4. Your uncle gives you a camera as a gift. You already have a much better camera. Besides, you don't like this kind of camera. What do you say to your uncle? (Many gifts today come with a gift receipt.)

Follow-up activity ❁

Look at the question below. Find out how two of your friends outside class would respond in this situation. Report their responses to your group or class.

Question: What do you say in this situation?

Your friend prepares a special dinner for your birthday. The food tastes terrible. You can hardly eat it. Your friend says, "I hope you're enjoying your birthday dinner." You say: "________________."

Friend 1: ____

Friend 2: ____

Five Things That Will Disappear in our Lifetime (in the U.S.)

full text on page 95 (cd track 3)

Introduction ❁

You may find some of these things surprising. Would these things also be true in your country? After you have done the dictation, check the items that surprise you!

Vocabulary, Pronunciation ❁

1. **junk mail**: useless mail; ads; stuff you throw away
2. **bills**: statements of charges that you have to pay, i.e. electric bill
3. **out of business**: no longer in service; discontinued
4. **subscribe**: to agree to receive and pay for a service for a period of time

Dictation ❁ *Listen and fill in the blanks with the words you hear.*

1. **The Post Office**

   Can you imagine a world ______________ _____ __________ _____________?

   They are in serious financial trouble _____________ _____ ___________,

   Federal Express (_________), and United Postal Service (________), which

   delivers packages. Every day most of our mail is __________ ___________

   ______ _____________.

2. **The Check**

   It costs the financial system ____________ ___ _______________ a year to

   process checks. This connects directly to the death _____ ________ ____________

   ___________. If you never __________ _________ ___________ _______

   ____________ and never received them by mail, the post office would definitely

   _____ _________ ______ _______________.

3. **The Land Line Telephone**

_______ _______ ________ ___________ __________________will let you make calls using the same cell provider ________ ________ _______________ against your minutes. If you have a large family and __________ ____ _______ ______ ______________ ___________, you may need a land line, but _____ _______ ______________ __________________________ for that extra service.

4. **The Newspaper**

People under 40 don't ___________ ________ _______________; they get their news online. Many don't subscribe to a daily delivered print edition. _______ ______________ ______ _______________ ________________ the paper online is due to the rise in Internet devices, and companies ________ ____________ ________ ______________ have developed a model for paid subscription services.

5. **Privacy**

Privacy ______ __________ ___________ for a long time. There are cameras on the street, ____ __________ ______________, and even built into your computer ____ _______ __________. You can be sure that 24/7, "they" know who you are ____ _________ ______ ______.

Discussion

With a partner, talk about these items.

1. Which items surprised you? Didn't surprise you? Explain.
2. What other changes do you see happening in the next 20 years? What kind of changes will there be? Comment on:

   a. Joined handwriting (cursive) b. internet services c. television
   d. music e. books and textbooks f. plane rides g. university courses
   h. (your ideas) ________________

3. Comment on what has appeared/disappeared in your parents', and/or grandparents' lifetime.

   a. disposable diapers (came into popularity in 1968). What did parents use before then?
   b. dishwashers (came on the market in the mid 1950s)
   c. computers (common usage began in the late 1980s)
   d. the Internet (became more prevalent in 2000)
   e. fax machines

Follow-up activity

Interview people over age 70 and ask the following questions:

Do you remember:

1. shopping without a credit card?
2. growing up with no TV in the house? when you got your first TV? how many channels there were?
3. having only one telephone in the house?
4. growing up with no car? how old you were when your family got a car?
5. walking everywhere?

Wild Turkeys

full text on page 96 (cd track 4)

Introduction ❁

Wild turkeys are everywhere! You can find them from California to New York, across the U.S.A. In 1959 there were about 350,000 of them, and they lived in the forests. Today there are over 7,000,000, and many of them are walking around in city streets. Can you find wild turkeys in the town or city where you live? Here is a story of a wild turkey that was waiting for a woman at a bus stop!

Vocabulary, Pronunciation ❁

1. **a honk:** a loud noise made with a car horn (or by a goose)
2. **to poke:** to push into something (with something sharp like a finger)
3. **to scream:** to make a very loud, high-pitched noise

Dictation ❁ *Fill in the blank spaces with the words you hear. With a partner, check your responses.*

People began to see wild turkeys in cities ____ ________ __________ ________. They were very excited and took lots of photos. Now that there are so many of these large birds, people are not so happy. Some people are afraid _____ __________. Here is a story about Mrs. Rosen.

One day Mrs. Rosen, ___ ______________, got off the bus ____ ______ _____ the bank in her city. She felt something poke _____ _____ ______ _______. She turned around and saw a big wild turkey. She began to run, and the turkey _______ _________ ______. At the bank, she turned around and screamed very loudly at the turkey, "________ ___________!" The turkey turned around and slowly started to cross the street. All traffic stopped. Cars honked _________ _________. The turkey didn't care. It wasn't _____ _____ __________. It walked very slowly until it got to the sidewalk.

One wildlife official said that if you run from turkeys as Mrs. Rosen did, ________ _______ ___________ _____ because they think it's a game.

Discussion ❁ *With a partner, discuss the following questions.*

1. Have you ever seen a wild turkey? Where?
2. What would you do if a wild turkey was following you?
3. What are some of the reasons that wild turkeys and other wild animals are moving into cities?
4. What wild animals have you seen in cities?
5. What do you think we should do about them?
6. Do you think that animals are as important as humans?

Follow-up activities ❁

1. *Find out about another wild animal that can now be found in suburbs or cities. Some examples are coyotes, raccoons, and hawks. Write a paragraph about the animal and also make a short presentation. Be sure to have a picture of the animal with you so that you can show it to the class.*
2. *On the internet, search for information on wild animals in urban habitats. Search suggestion: wild animals city. Report on your discoveries.*

Tipping in a Restaurant

full text on page 97 (cd track 5)

Introduction ❁

When you are eating out in a restaurant in the U.S. or Canada, the custom is to leave a tip for the server. The standard tip is 15–20%.

Dictation ❁ *Here is a chart to help you figure out what the tip should be. Listen and write the amount in the chart.*

Check	15%	20%
$20.00	3.00	4.00
$35.00	5.25	_____
$58.00	_____	11.60
_____	10.80	_____
$86.00	_____	17.20
_____	14.55	_____

Discussion ❁ *Talk about these situations with a partner. Share your responses with the class.*

1. You are finished with dinner. The waiter brings the check. It's for $66. You want to pay cash, so you add a $10 tip. The waiter sees you are ready to pay and asks, "Do you want any change?" What do you say?
   a. Yes, please! b. No, it's all set.

2. You give the waitress a $50 bill for a $30 dinner. When she asks, "Do you want any change?" what do you say?

3. If you only have two twenty-dollar bills for the $25 dinner, what will you do? How much tip will you leave? If you sit for two hours with friends for lunch, do you leave a higher tip? Why or why not?

Follow-up activities ❁

What percent should you leave a hairdresser, a taxi driver, a hotel bellhop, a pizza delivery person, a manicurist, or a newspaper delivery person as a tip? Ask several people, or do an internet search for tipping etiquette.

Changing Careers

full text on page 98 (cd track 6)

Introduction ❁

"I'm my own boss. I feel healthier and happier than I ever did before," says Terry Meyers, a woman who started her own small business after many years in the medical profession.

Vocabulary, Pronunciation ❁

1. **to borrow**: to use something that belongs to someone else and give it back
2. **items**: things
3. **paws**: dogs' feet

Work with a partner and read the sentences that describe Terry Meyers and her working life before she made a big career change. Put the sentences in chronological or logical order, from 1 to 8.

_______ In 2004 she quit her job to start her own business.

_______ However, she couldn't find a university teaching job.

_______ After getting her bachelor's degree, she worked in a hospital laboratory for six months.

___1___ She was born near New York City.

_______ So she joined a company and sold medical instruments.

_______ When she was 18, she studied science at the State University of New York in Buffalo.

_______ Because she wanted to teach in a university, she left her job in the laboratory and went back to the University of Minnesota to get a Master's degree in Medical Microbiology.

_______ She finally moved to Massachusetts to begin an important job in a large company and worked there for over 20 years.

Dictation ❁ *Fill in the blank spaces with the words you hear. With a partner, check your responses.*

In __________ a friend gave Terry a __________ __________ as a gift. She named him Kanji. Terry's life changed. She had __________ __________ ________ earlier to take care of Kanji. He made her feel better. She was healthier and happier.

In __________ she decided it was time for a change. She quit her __________ and decided to open a store that sold things for dogs and cats. She had saved __________ __________ __________ __________ so she didn't have to borrow any. For a year she went to classes on how to start a small business. Then she found a __________ empty store near ________ __________.

A well-dressed Scottie dog in boots

She __________ many useful things and many things that are not as useful. One of her best-selling items __________ __________ is rubber boots that look like balloons. They are important in the winter so that dogs don't get sand and salt in their paws when they __________ on icy streets. She also ________ things like ____________ jackets __________ __________ and T-shirts that say, "Dogs are children in fur coats." She says that she __________ _________ ________ happier.

Discussion ❁ *With a partner, discuss the following questions.*

1. Do you think that Terry Meyers did the right thing when she quit her job? She had a high position, earned a high salary, and traveled around the world.

2. What do you think are the good things and the bad things about owning a small business?

3. If you could start a small business, what kind of business would you start?

4. Terry has brought her sister into the business. What do you think are the good things and bad things about a family business?

5. With a partner, decide if each of the following is useful, not useful, or both. Write "U" for useful, "NU" for not useful, or "B" for both.

    __________ 1. a box of chocolates in a red heart-shaped box
    __________ 2. a wool scarf
    __________ 3. a set of beautiful expensive dishes
    __________ 4. a fur coat
    __________ 5. pink nail polish
    __________ 6. dog toys
    __________ 7. an iPod

Follow-up activities ❁

1. *Here are some dog idioms and expressions. Find the meanings of these expressions by asking people or checking a dictionary.*

    1. We're in the dog days of summer.
    2. You can't teach an old dog new tricks.
    3. He's as sick as a dog.
    4. It's raining cats and dogs.
    5. Let sleeping dogs lie.
    6. I'll take a doggy bag.
    7. It's a dog's life.

2. *Be sure to go to the "Cause to Paws" website,* www.causetopaws.com, *to see Terry and Kanji.*

Greeting Cards

full text on page 99 (cd track 7)

Introduction ❁

Before 1859, a greeting card was an expensive, handmade gift which had to be delivered by hand. After 1859 greeting cards became popular because there were advances in printing and the postage stamp was introduced.

Vocabulary, Pronunciation ❁

1. **amazing**: surprising
2. **nineteen ten**: 1910
3. **nineteen thousand**: 19,000
4. **same-sex marriage**: marriage between two men or two women
5. **serious**: not funny
6. **sympathy**: being sorry for someone who is in a bad situation
7. **unfortunately**: It was too bad.
8. **Why not?**: OK or Yes

Dictation ❁ *Fill in the blank spaces with the words you hear. With a partner, check your responses.*

Hallmark ________ ________ ________ greeting card company ________ ________ ________ ________. The company started ________ ________. It makes about ________ ________ ________ a year. About ________ people ________ for the company. The average person sends about ________ ________ a year.

Now ________ ________ ________ musical cards that ________ ________ like "Happy Birthday to You" when you open them. You can ________ ________ electronic greeting cards (e-cards) or send greetings to a mobile ________ by text message.

In August ________ Hallmark began ________ ________ same-sex marriage cards for states where same-sex marriage is legal.

The company's motto is "When you care enough to send ________ ________ ________."

Listening ❁

Listen to the conversation between a shopper and a man who is interviewing shoppers in a greeting card store. Then write "T" for true and "F" for false next to the statements that you hear on the CD.

___ 1. The shopper says that she sends about 55 cards a year.

___ 2. The shopper says that she spends about $2.95 for every card.

___ 3. The shopper says that she sent a St. Valentine's Day card the previous week.

___ 4. The man asking the questions is very polite.

___ 5. The shopper is probably young.

Discussion ❁ *With a partner, discuss the following questions.*

1. Do you send cards? What kind? Who do you send cards to?
2. Do you like to receive them? What do you do with them?
3. Do you buy, or do you make cards? Why?

Follow-up activities ❁

Do one or several of the activities. When you have finished, present your information to the class.

1. Interview five people. Ask them these questions:

   a. About how many Christmas cards do you send every year?
   b. Have you ever sent an electronic card?
   c. Would you rather receive an electronic card or a card in the mail? Why?
   d. Have you ever made a card for someone and given it to him or her?
   e. Do you keep all of the cards you receive?
   f. Have you ever received a card that plays music?

2. Go to a store that sells cards. Make a list of all the kinds of cards they have. Present your information to the class.

3. Make a card for someone. Show it to the class, and talk about it before you send it.

4. Bring to class a card that is not in English.
   Talk to the class about where it is from, and translate it.

5. Write about a time when you received or sent a card. You can write about who the card was for or from, about how you chose the card, about how you felt when you received the card, or any other thing you can think of relating to the card.

Trivia Contests

full text on page 100 (cd track 8)

Introduction ❁

Trivia is information that is not important but is fun to know.

Vocabulary, Pronunciation ❁

1. **a contest**: a game
2. **to fly**: to travel by plane
3. **a buck**: a U.S. dollar
4. **a whopper**: something big, specifically a hamburger
5. **junior**: younger or smaller

Dictation ❁

Listen and fill in the blank spaces with the words you hear. Then work together in pairs or small groups, and answer all of the questions, even if you have to guess. The group with the most correct answers wins the contest.

1. Where can _______ __________ a Whopper Junior?
2. Who ______________ *Romeo and Juliet*?
3. What language do ____________ _____ Mexico speak?
4. How much does a pack of cigarettes _____________?
5. Where is the longest _____________ in the world located?
6. How long _________ it __________ to fly from New York to London?
7. How much is __________ _______________?
8. What does "I _______ _______" mean?
9. Where are the next Summer Olympics ___________ _____ _____?
10. _______ _______ invited to a potluck party. What does potluck mean?

Discussion ❁

A quiz for your teacher and your classmates! Work in groups of three. Write some questions about students in your class, or about your school or culture, that you think others can answer. Practice using questions with WH or How much/many. Then, working with another group, ask your questions and answer theirs. Here are two sample questions:

1. How many students in this class are from (Mexico/Turkey/Albania)?
2. Who comes to class by bus?

Follow-up activities ❁

Fact and Opinion

1. *A fact is a generally accepted statement of truth that can be checked in a dictionary, encyclopedia, or other reference source. An opinion, on the other hand, expresses a personal feeling, idea, or point of view. Write F or O next to each statement.*

___ 1. There are 50 states in the United States.
___ 2. California has the best weather.
___ 3. McDonald's is a good place to eat.
___ 4. There are McDonald's in many countries of the world.
___ 5. The Summer Olympic Games are every four years.
___ 6. Ice skating is the best Olympic sport to watch on television.
___ 7. People in 20 different countries speak Spanish.
___ 8. Spanish is an easy language to learn.
___ 9. Cigarettes can cause cancer.
___ 10. Cigarettes are too expensive.

Top Five

2. *Find out the top five in each category.*

    1. The five largest countries in area.
    2. The five largest countries in population.
    3. The five countries with the longest life expectancies.
    4. The five car-producing companies.
    5. The five countries with the most people per household (the largest families).

Languages in the U.S.

full text on page 101 (cd track 9)

Introduction ❁

The United States is a country with many languages. Most people speak English, of course, but there are 311 other languages that people speak. Of the 311, 162 are indigenous languages and 149 are immigrant languages. An indigenous language is a language that is native to a region and spoken by indigenous people like Native American Indians. Can you name some languages that immigrants in the U.S. speak?

Vocabulary, Pronunciation ❁

1. **the Census Bureau**: a government agency that counts the population
2. **the population**: the number of people living in one area
3. **a household**: a home
4. **an immigrant**: a person who comes to the U.S. to live permanently
5. **nationwide**: across the country

Dictation ❁ *Fill in the blank spaces with the words you hear. With a partner, check your responses.*

The population of the United States ____ 325,000,000. Most people speak English, but the Census Bureau tells us that _________ _______ 14 million U.S. households where people speak ___ _________________ other than English. In the state of California, more than _______ language is spoken in 40% of the households _______________. Nationwide, one in five children enters _______________ speaking a language other than English.

Unfortunately, these __________________ often lose much of their first language when they _______________ _______________. When immigrant students are in high school and have been in the U.S. since they were ______ or ______, many of them can still ____________________ their first language, but they cannot read _____ __________________ in their first language.

Discussion

Look at the chart and answer these questions with a partner.

Top 15 Languages Spoken in the U.S.

(The total U.S. population at present is about 325,000,000. English is spoken by over 80% of people over 5 years old. Languages other than English are spoken by about 20%. The following statistics are approximate.)

Language	Speakers	Percentage
English	260,000,000	80%
Spanish	39,000,000	12%
Chinese	2,150,000	0.66%
Tagalog	1,720,000	0.53%
Vietnamese	1,500,000	0.46%
French	1,400,000	0.44%
Korean	1,200,000	0.38%
German	1,200,000	0.38%
Russian	945,000	0.29%
Arabic	845,000	0.26%
Italian	845,000	0.26%
Portuguese	780,000	0.24%
Haitian Creole	750,000	0.23%
Polish	682,000	0.21%
Hindi	650,000	0.20%

1. How many Spanish speakers are there in the U.S.?
2. What is the percentage of Arabic speakers?
3. How many Asian languages are listed?
4. What language groups have more than 1,000,000 speakers?
5. What is the percentage of Hindi speakers?
6. How many people speak Haitian Creole?
7. How many European languages are on this chart?
8. What are some other languages not on this list that you know about?
9. In what country is Tagalog the first language?
10. What languages are spoken by the same percentage of people?

Follow-up activities

1. Name 10 countries where __________ is spoken as the first language.
   a. Spanish b. English c. Arabic
2. Is it important for young immigrants to maintain fluency in their first language? Explain your opinion.
3. Do a search "Languages spoken in the U.S." and compare the numbers of:
   a. Spanish speakers in 2010 and 2014 b. Chinese speakers in 2010 and 2014

Valentine's Day Around the World

full text on page 102 (cd track 10)

Introduction ❁

Valentine's Day is a special day in the United States and many countries around the world. Below are some countries that celebrate Valentine's Day. Not every country or person celebrates it in the same way, of course, but giving chocolates, gifts, cards, and flowers is what most people in the U.S. and Canada do. Is that true for you?

Vocabulary, Pronunciation ❁

1. **to celebrate**: to do something special (for example, have a party)
2. **cookies**: small, flat, sweet cakes
3. **a gift**: something you give to another; a present

Dictation ❁

Fill in the blank spaces with the words you hear. With a partner, check your answers and talk about them.

1. **The Dominican Republic and El Salvador**

   In these countries, friends and family _________ ___________. In the Dominican Republic, _______ __________ is called *Angelito,* and in El Salvador it is called *Amigo Secreto* (secret friend). Friends write ______ ________ of another person (boy or girl) on a small piece of paper. Then each player _________ this friend a ___________.

2. **Italy and Britain**

   Young women stand by ________ ___________ in the early morning on Valentine's Day. They believe that ________ _________ _________ they see will be their husband!

3. **Japan**

   Japan ________ ________ Valentine's Days. On February 14th, ________ _______ dark chocolate to the boys _________ _________, and on March 14th, ________ ______ cookies or ________ chocolate to the girls they like.

Discussion ❁

Work with a partner, and answer these questions. Share your responses with the class.

1. If your country is not mentioned in this unit, tell the class
   a. if you have this special day, what customs do you follow?
   b. if you don't have this day, what other holiday do you celebrate?

2. Valentine's Day is a big day for candy stores. What other stores do a big business on this day?

3. A Valentine's Day Poem. Practice this with your class.

Roses are red,
Violets are blue,
Sugar is sweet,
And so are you!

Now finish the poem with your line.

Roses are red,
Violets are blue,
Sugar is sweet,
____

Follow-up activity ❁

You will find these expresions printed on candy hearts. To find out what they mean, ask an American friend.

1. Be Mine!	2. True Love	3. 100 Hugs	4. Love me!	5. Kiss Me!
6. Marry me!	7. Call Me!	8. Cutie Pie	9. Lover Boy	10. Smile!

The Youngest College Professor

full text on page 103 (cd track 11)

Introduction ✣

Alia Sabur is an amazing woman. She was appointed to teach physics and math as a college professor at Southern University in New Orleans, Louisiana. Why was this big news? Because Alia was only 19 years old!

Vocabulary, Pronunciation ✣

1. **amazing**: surprising
2. **to graduate**: to receive an academic degree from a high school or university
3. **a Master's degree**: a college degree above a Bachelor's
4. **a Ph.D.**: a Doctor of Philosophy degree; an advanced university degree above a Master's

Dictogloss ✣ *Listen to a complete sentence only once. Write down the words you can remember. With a partner, try to reconstruct the sentence in writing as accurately as possible.*

1.

2.

3.

Dictation ✣ *Write the correct word or words in the blank space.*

When Alia graduated from Stony Brook University in New York, _____ ______ the youngest woman in U.S. history to do so. Her education continued at Drexel University _____ Pennsylvania, where _______ ________________her Master's and a Ph.D. in materials science and engineering. She ___________ ___________ because she feels she can help ____ _________ ____ people.

Discussion ✣

Talk about these items with a partner, and share your answers with the class.

1. At what age do most children _______?
   a. begin school b. learn to read

2. At what age do students usually graduate from ______?
   a. high school b. college

3. At what age did Alia graduate from ________?
   a. high school b. college

4. What problems, if any, might a woman like Alia have ______?
   a. in her social life b. in her professional life

5. Alia is also good at playing the clarinet, and she has a black belt in *tae kwon do.* People like Alia are called <u>*prodigies*</u>. A <u>*prodigy*</u> is a super intelligent person who can do things well. There are children like this in every country. Do you know of any?

Discussion ✣

Don't be fooled! Here are some brain teasers. Work with a partner and see if you can get the answers. *Answers are on page 103.*

Example: When the Vice-President of the U.S. dies, who is the President?
Answer: The President!

1. A girl who was just learning to drive went down a one-way street in the wrong direction, but didn't break the law. Why not?

2. Why do Chinese men eat more rice than Japanese men do?

3. Bobby's mother had four children. The first was April, the second was May, and the third was June. What was the name of the fourth child?

4. How many months have 28 days?

Follow-up activity ✣

Find a funny riddle or brain teaser and tell it to the class.

How Green Are You?

full text on page 104 (cd track 12)

Introduction ✣

Are you green? If you are, you think it is important to protect the environment. You want your children to grow up in a healthy world. Name a few things you already do to help save our planet.

Vocabulary, Pronunciation ✣

1. **a hybrid**: a car that runs on both gasoline and electricity
2. **purchases**: the things we buy
3. **to recycle**: to save things and use them again
4. **waste**: the things we throw away

Dictation (a) ✣ *Write the words you hear in the blank space.*

1. With your car:

   I don't __________. I take the bus _____ ______________ to work.

2. With your food:

   I eat more vegetables _______ ________________than I used to.

3. With your waste:

   I recycle newspapers, _______________, ______________, and plastic.

4. With your purchases:

   I try to buy products that __________ environmentally friendly, even if they are ____________ ______________________.

Dictogloss (b) ✣ *Listen only once. Write what you can remember. With a partner, try to reconstruct the sentence and write it down. Check the items that you already do, and discuss with a partner.*

1.

2.

3.

4.

Discussion ✣

Work with a partner and talk about the following. Share your answers with the class.

1. Ways to save water in your home:

    a.

    b.

    c.

2. Ways to save electricity:

    a.

    b.

    c.

3. Ways to save paper:

    a.

    b.

    c.

4. Ways to have cleaner air:

    a.

    b.

    c.

Follow-up activity ✣

Ask two students outside of your class these questions. Bring your responses to class and share them.

Question	*Student 1*	*Student 2*
1. Would you buy a hybrid car? Why or why not? 2. What is one thing you are doing in your home to help save the environment?		

Kissing

full text on page 105 (cd track 13)

Introduction ✣

There are many reasons to kiss. In modern Western culture a kiss usually shows affection. But we also kiss on the cheek when we greet friends.

Vocabulary, Pronunciation ✣

1. **affection**: gentle feeling of love and caring
2. **an anthropologist**: someone who studies people and their societies
3. **a beak**: the pointed mouth of a bird
4. **to chew**: to bite food several times
5. **to greet**: to say hello to someone or welcome them
6. **a primate**: a member of the group of mammals that includes humans and apes

Dictation ✣ *Fill in the blank spaces with the words you hear. With a partner, check your answers.*

Anthropologists think that kissing began with ________-to-____________

feeding of primates by their mothers. ___________________ may have chewed

____________ ___________ first and then _____________ ___________ in their

babies' mouths. Mother birds __________ _________ __________ food in their beaks.

This is called beak-to-beak feeding. ___________ _____________ see this as kissing.

Dictogloss ✣ *Listen to a complete sentence only once and write down the words you can remember. With a partner, try to reconstruct the sentence in writing as accurately as possible.*

1.

2.

3.

4.

Discussion ✣

With a partner, discuss the following questions.

1. It is common in some countries to greet people by kissing them on the cheek. How do you greet people in your country?

2. There are popular kissing games that children play, like "Spin the Bottle" or "Post Office." Have you ever played a kissing game at a party?

3. In children's stories (fairy tales and folktales) a kiss is often an important part of the story. For example, in *Sleeping Beauty* the wicked witch puts the princess to sleep for a long time. It is only when the handsome prince kisses her that she comes to life again. Can you think of any story in your first language or in English where a kiss is important?

Sleeping Beauty

Follow-up activity ✣

1. *With your partner, make up a list of five questions to ask people about kissing. You can start with the first two questions here or make up five of your own. Ask three people your questions.*

   a. Do you kiss with your eyes open or closed?

   b. Can you remember your first romantic kiss?

   c. ______________________________?

   d. ______________________________?

   e. ______________________________?

2. *Kiss idioms and expressions: Find the meanings of these expressions by asking people or checking a dictionary.*

   a. I'm sorry. Let's kiss and make up.
   b. If you leave your purse on that desk, you can kiss it goodbye.
   c. He blew her a kiss from the train window.
   d. He bought a small bag of chocolate kisses to eat at the theater.

Soap Operas

full text on page 106 (cd track 14)

Introduction ✣

Soap opera is the name for TV dramas which continue for weeks, months, and even years. We call them soap operas because the companies that advertised on these programs made soap for washing clothes, dishes, or faces. The people who watched these programs were housewives. One popular program was General Hospital, which was on for 43 years from 1964 to 2007.

Vocabulary, Pronunciation ✣

1. **to advertise**: to persuade people to buy or use something
2. **clothes**: pronounce like "close (the door)"
3. **a housewife**: a married woman who does not have a job outside the house
4. **an arranged marriage**: a marriage in which the parents choose a husband or wife for their child

Dictation ✣ *Fill in the blank spaces with the words you hear. With a partner, check your answers.*

Soap operas are popular _____ countries ______ ____________ ______ ______________.
For example, people ________ __________ _____________ and Korea enjoy watching Korean soap operas. People in ______________ Turkey and Greece ______________ watching Turkish soap operas.

India _________ _____________ ____________ operas in _____________ different languages. _________ became popular in the late 1980's as more people _______________ ______ ___________ televisions. At ______ _______________________ of the 21st century, soap operas ________________ an important part of Indian culture. _______________ ________ _________________ are about ______________________ and ______________________ _____________.

Dictogloss ✣ *Listen to a complete sentence only once and write down the words you can remember on a separate piece of paper. With a partner, try to reconstruct the entire sentence and write it below.*

1.

2.

3.

Discussion ✣

With a partner, discuss these questions.

1. Do you like soap operas? Do you have a favorite program? Is it in English or in your first language?
2. Why do you think soap operas are so popular?
3. Do you think that more women watch soap operas than men? Why?

Follow-up activity ✣

Punctuation

Punctuation marks are marks used to divide a piece of writing into sentences. This little story from a soap opera is missing the punctuation and capital letters that it needs. For example, period (.) comma (,) question mark (?). Can you and your partner put them in? When you are done, tell what you think will happen next.

tiffany loves derek but derek only loves tiffany like a sister he loves claudia she is not a very good woman and only likes derek because he has a lot of money it is may derek and claudia are going to have a big wedding in june they have invited three hundred people will tiffany come to the wedding

Traffic

full text on page 107 (cd track 15)

Introduction ✣

Traffic is a problem in many cities. Drivers in one third of U.S. cities spend more than forty hours a year in traffic that is not moving. Is traffic a problem in your city?

1 kilometer	=	0.6214 miles
35 km	=	22 miles
110 km	=	65 miles
200 km	=	119 miles

Vocabulary, Pronunciation ✣

1. **a cop**: a policeman or policewoman
2. **to honk**: to blow a car horn
3. **MPH**: miles per hour
4. **the speed limit**: how fast you are allowed to go

Dictation ✣

The following dictation is a joke about driving and traffic. Fill in the blank spaces with the words you hear. Try to understand why the joke is funny. Then read the joke out loud with your partner. One of you should be the woman, and one of you should be the police officer.

A cop pulls over a carload of women from another country.

Cop: This is a _________ MPH highway. Why _____ _____ _________ so slowly?

Woman: Sir, I saw a lot of signs that said 22, not 65.

Cop: That's not the speed limit. ________ _____ ___________ of the highway you're on.

Woman: Oh! Silly me! ________ for letting me know. I'll be more careful.

At this point the cop looks in the backseat, where the other women are shaking and trembling.

Cop: Excuse me, _____________ ____________ _________ your friends back there? They're shaking terribly.

Woman: Oh, we just got off of Highway _______.

Dictogloss ✣

Listen to a complete sentence only once and write down the words you can remember on a separate piece of paper. With a partner, try to reconstruct the entire sentence and write it below.

1.

2.

3.

Discussion ✣

Discuss these questions with a partner. Share your ideas with the class.

1. Is traffic a problem in your city or in a city that you've lived in?
2. How do you get to school, work, or home? How long does it take you?
3. What do you do to keep from getting upset when you're stuck in traffic?
4. Do you have any ideas for how cities could improve the traffic situation?

Follow-up activity ✣

Write about one of the following.

A Good (or bad) Driving Experience
A Good (or bad) Bus or Subway Experience
Public Transportation in My City

Oprah's School in South Africa

full text on page 108 (cd track 16)

Introduction ✣

Oprah Winfrey is the famous billionaire American talk show host, actress, TV producer, and philanthropist. In 2007, she opened a school for 500 girls in South Africa called the Oprah Winfrey Leadership Academy. It cost $40,000,000 to build and is open to girls in grades 7 to 12. The first graduating class was in 2011 and consisted of 72 girls who earned full college scholarships to schools in the U.S. and South Africa.

Vocabulary, Pronunciation ✣

1. **to apply: to** ask for admission to a school
2. **an interview**: to get information by asking questions
3. **a leader:** a person who directs others
4. **tuition**: the cost of going to a school

Dictation ✣ *Listen and write the word or words you hear in the blank spaces. With a partner, check your answers.*

The Oprah Winfrey Leadership Academy _____ ___________ ______ poor girls who want _____ ___________ and become leaders. Classes at the school _______ ___________, with only 15 students. Teachers come from _______ ________________ countries to share their knowledge and ideas. The school has _____ _________________, including computer and science labs, dormitories, and a health center. Tuition ______ ____________.

Dictogloss ✣ *Listen to a complete sentence only once and write down the words you can remember. With a partner, try to reconstruct the sentence in writing as accurately as possible.*

1.

2.

3.

Discussion ✣

Choose one or more of these topics and talk about them with a partner. Share your ideas with the class.

1. Oprah was a poor girl who grew up with her grandmother in Mississippi. She had no water or electricity in the home, like many of these South African girls. She built the school because of her respect for Nelson Mandela and her own African roots. Oprah hopes these girls will be able to attend any university in the world when they graduate from her school. What kinds of problems do you think these girls might have?

2. Many of the girls come from families affected by HIV/AIDS. Why is the health center important?

3. Oprah says, "When you educate a girl, you begin to change the face of a nation." What does this mean?

4. Oprah has a lot of money to give away to people and organizations who need it. If you were Oprah and had money to give away, who would you give it to?

5. Good teachers are important in every school. Here are some characteristics of a good teacher. Which ones do you think are the most important? Explain why.

    *cares about the students
    *is friendly, patient, and kind *(patient: calm; not in a hurry)*
    *can explain clearly
    *is strict *(strict: expects students to follow rules)*
    *prepares you for state tests
    *knows the subject very well
    *knows the answers to all of the students' questions
    *gives easy tests

Follow-up activities ✣

Write about one of the following topics:

1. Remember a favorite teacher you had in school.

2. Tell the class if it is possible for a poor but smart person in your country to go to a university.

Overworked

full text on page 109 (cd track 17)

Introduction ✣

Do you work hard? Do you enjoy your job? Would you like more vacation time? These are important questions for people, because we often work for fifty years of our lives.

Vocabulary, Pronunciation ✣

1. **overwork**: working too long and too hard
2. **a workweek**: the number of hours a person works in a week

Dictation ✣ *Write the words you hear in the blank spaces. With a partner, check your answers.*

Karoshi is the Japanese phrase for "death from ____________." Thirty years ago the Japanese government ____________ that workers who work for ________ ________ ________ ________ a day, six or seven ____________ ______ ______, year ________ ________, might die from overwork. A government officer can decide if the person died from overwork. Then the family will be paid money. South Koreans, who have the ____________ ____________ ____________ in the world, call death by work *kwarosa*.

Dictogloss ✣ *Listen to a complete sentence only once and write down the words you can remember. With a partner, try to reconstruct the sentence and write it below.*

1.

2.

3.

International business means long hours.

Discussion ✣

With a partner, discuss the following questions.

1. How many hours a week do people in your country generally work?
2. Are there laws in your country about working hours and length of vacation?
3. There are people who choose to work more than 40 hours a week. Can you think about who these people might be?
4. What are some of the advantages and disadvantages of working long hours?
5. What do you think would be perfect work hours?
6. Do you know what the letters TGIF stand for?
7. Do most workers in your country get pensions and health benefits from their employers?
8. Do many workers in your country travel long distances to get to their jobs?

Follow-up activity ✣

Choose one of the following topics to write about.

1. Write about a job you had that you loved (or hated). Describe the job and tell why you loved (or hated) it.
2. Write about what you think the best job in the world is and/or what you think the worst job in the world is.

Stay-At-Home Dads

full text on page 110 (cd track 18)

Introduction

More and more fathers are staying home with their young children while their wives go off to work every morning. Can you think of three reasons why this is happening?

Vocabulary, Pronunciation

1. **to raise**: to help a child grow up
2. **twins**: two children born to the same mother at the same time
3. **a salary**: pay for the work you do
4. **day care:** a business that takes care of pre-school children

Pre-listening Dictogloss

Listen to a sentence only once and write down the words you can remember. With a partner, try to reconstruct the sentence in writing as accurately as possible.

1. ______________________________
2. ______________________________
3. ______________________________

Listening

Listen to the conversation between Jack, a stay-at-home dad, and the interviewer. Then write "T" for true and "F" for false next to the following statements that you hear on the CD.

___ 1. It was an easy decision for Jack to stay at home.

___ 2. Day care centers are too expensive for Jack and his wife.

___ 3. Jack thinks children are happier at home with a parent.

___ 4. His wife makes a pretty good salary.

___ 5. Jack used to work as a teacher.

___ 6. Living on one salary is not working out.

___ 7. His wife was happy to go back to work.

___ 8. Jack plans to go back to work when the twins go to school.

___ 9. Being a full-time dad at home is easy.

___ 10. When he goes back to work, his wife will stay home.

A stay-at-home father feeding his son.

Discussion

With a partner, discuss the following questions

1. What is the role of the father in your culture or family? Is this a comfortable situation for everyone?
2. Do you see any changes in the role of fathers in the near future?
3. What are some typical "women's jobs" that men are now doing? What are some typical "men's jobs" that women are now doing?
4. Do you celebrate a *Father's Day* or a *Mother's Day*? If yes, how do you spend the day?

Follow-up activity

1. *Here are some expressions for mothers and fathers. Find out what they mean by asking people or using a dictionary (online or not).*

Mothers	***Fathers***
mother tongue	Father Time
Mother Nature	father figure
motherless	fatherless
motherhood	fatherland
godmother	godfather
mother-in-law	father-in-law
stepmother	stepfather

2. *Make a list of occupations that allow people to work at home. Share them with the class.*

A Courageous Athlete

full text on page 111 (cd track 19)

Introduction

Over the past 50 years there have been more and more opportunities for athletes with physical disabilities. In 1975 one push-rim wheelchair racer finished the 26-mile Boston Marathon. This changed the way we saw people with disabilities. Now many wheelchair athletes compete in marathons around the world and we admire them for their strength and courage.

Vocabulary, Pronunciation

1. **to compete**: (competition) to try to win, to try to be more successful
2. **courage**: (courageous) brave
3. **a disability**: a physical condition that makes it difficult to do what most people can do
4. **a marathon**: a 26-mile race
5. **paralyzed**: unable to move part or all of your body
6. **the spine**: the column of bones down the center of your back
7. **strength**: (strengthen) strong
8. **a wheelchair**: a chair with wheels used by people who cannot walk. The wheel on a push-rim wheelchair is pushed by hand.

Dictation ✣ *Write the correct word or words in the blank space. With a partner, check your answers.*

In ________ Tatyana McFadden, a talented 24-year-old disabled athlete, became __________ ______________ ______________ ________ _________ all four major marathons _____ _____ ___________. (________________, __________________, Chicago, ______ __________ ________). In 2014 she won the Boston marathon again.

She _________ ___________ in Russia in 1988 with spina bifida (a hole in her spine), which left her paralyzed ______________ _______ ______________. For the _______ _______ _________ of her life she had _______ ______________ on her hands _______ _________ _________ because she lived in a poor orphanage and didn't have a wheelchair.

In 1994 she was adopted by Debbie McFadden, an American, and began to _______ ______________ ______________ like swimming and gymnastics to strengthen her muscles. She has competed in many________________, has won many medals, and _________ _____________ ____________ active in ________________ disabled athletes _________ the right to compete.

Dictogloss ✣ *Listen only once. Write what you can remember. With a partner, try to reconstruct the sentence and write it down as accurately as possible.*

1.

2.

3.

Discussion ✣ *Work with a partner and share your answers with the class.*

1. Have you ever run in or watched a marathon? Why do people run marathons?
2. What new technologies are there that allow people with disabilities to do many things they couldn't do before?
3. There are other disabilities, like blindness (not being able to see). What other disabilities are there?

Follow-up activity ✣

1. Tatyana McFadden has had an interesting life. Find out more about her and present your information to the class.
2. There are many talented disabled athletes. Find out about one of them. Present your information to the class.
3. There are many special games for disabled athletes to compete in. Find out about these and present your information to the class.

Are You a Shopaholic?

full text on page 112 (cd track 20)

Introduction ❀

Sometimes we shop because we really need what we are going to buy. Sometimes we shop because we're bored. Can you think of other reasons why we sometimes shop?

Vocabulary, Pronunciation ❀

1. **bored**: tired because you think something is not interesting
2. **a closet**: an area where you keep clothes and other things
3. **a shopaholic**: a compulsive shopper who cannot control shopping
4. **window shopping**: looking at things without intending to buy them

Pair Dictation ❀ Student A

Work in pairs and dictate to each other. Student A has half of the dictation and reads their lines to Student B, who has the other half. A dictates and B writes; then Student B dictates and A writes, until the dictation is complete. With your partner, correct the dictation.

1. When I feel __________, I often go ______________.
2. I spend _____ ______ ______ __________ that I do not have _____ ________ that I do not need.
3. ________ ________ _________ full of clothes _______ _______ __________ never wear.
4. I feel _______ ________ and happy _______ _____ _______ something, _________ ________ ___ _____ tired and sad.
5. I often don't tell ________ _________ and my friends __________ _____ ________ I spent, _______ _____ _______ ______ that I have spent less ________ ____ _________ ______.

Pair Dictation ❀ Student B

Work in pairs and dictate to each other. Student A has half of the dictation and reads their lines to Student B, who has the other half. A dictates and B writes; then Student B dictates and A writes, until the dictation is complete. With your partner, correct the dictation.

1. _________ ______ _________ sad, _____ ________ _____ shopping.
2. ______ ____________ a lot of money ___________ ______ ______ _________ ___________ on things _________ _____ _______ ________ ___________.
3. I have closets __________ ______ ___________ that I almost _________ ________.
4. _______ ____________ very excited ______ ___________ when I buy _____________, but soon I feel ___________ _______ ________.
5. ______ ______________ __________ __________ my family _______ ______ _____________ about how much _____ ________, or I tell them ___________ _______ ___________ ____________ __________ than I really have.

Discussion

Discuss the following questions with your partner.

Do you enjoy shopping?

1. Which do you enjoy more
   - shopping in a large mall or on a street of separate small shops?
   - shopping with someone or shopping alone?
   - buying things for yourself or gifts for other people?
2. Do you enjoy an afternoon of window shopping even if you don't buy anything?
3. Do you buy "brand-name" goods because it makes you feel richer?
4. Guess what the following words mean.
   Do you know anyone who is _____________?
   - a shopaholic
   - a chocoholic
   - a netaholic
   - an alcoholic
   - a workaholic

Follow-up activities

*Write about **one** of the following topics.*

1. Are you a spender or a saver? Explain your choice. Give specific examples.
2. Describe your favorite store, shopping area, or mall.
3. What's the best way to teach children the value of money?
4. How did your parents teach you the value of money? Do you think they did a good job?

Three Wishes

full text on page 112 (cd track 21)

Introduction

Many children's stories are fairy tales. In this kind of story, a magical person often gives the hero or heroine several wishes. For example, in the Arabian fairy tale *Aladdin and the Magic Lamp,* Aladdin is given several wishes. This happens in fairy tales in many cultures. Here are three unusual wishes for you.

Vocabulary, Pronunciation

1. **at no cost**: free
2. **a fairy tale**: a story in which magical things happen. *Cinderella* is a fairy tale.
3. **a hero** (m) or **heroine** (f): the main character in a story
4. **a package**: something wrapped so it can be sent by mail

Pair Dictation ❀ Student A

Work in pairs and dictate to each other. Student A has half of the dictation and reads their lines to Student B, who has the other half. A dictates and B writes; then Student B dictates and A writes, until the dictation is complete. With your partner, correct the dictation.

1. You are studying English ____ ____ __________ __________. Choose a third language that __________ __________ _________. In a few days _______ ________ _____ ________ to listen to, __________, __________, and write this language well. What language _______ _______ __________, and why?
2. __________ __________ __________ a package ______ ____________. Decide who it will be from _________ ____________ what will be __________ _________.
3. ____________ __________ you can go ____________ in the world_________ _______ someone ________ _________. Where will you go, _________ _______ will you take _________ ___________?

Pair Dictation ❀ Student B

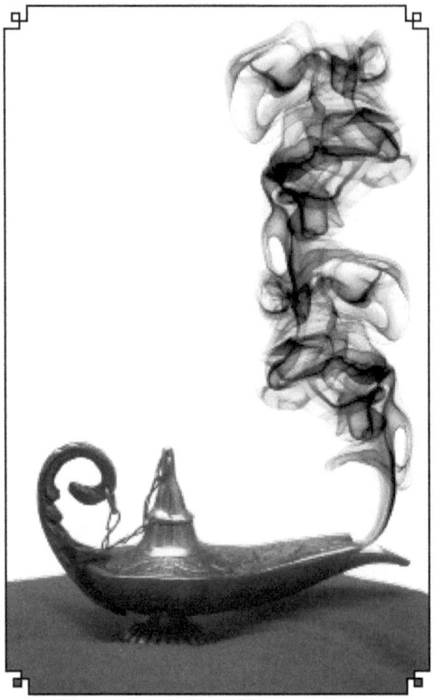

Work in pairs and dictate to each other. Student A has half of the dictation and reads their lines to Student B, who has the other half. A dictates and B writes; then Student B dictates and A writes, until the dictation is complete. With your partner, correct the dictation.

1. __________ __________ __________ __________ as a Second Language. __________ ___ __________ __________ __________ you don't know. _____ ____ __________ _________ you will be able ________ __________ _____, speak, read, _______ __________ _______ _______________ _______. _________ _________ will you choose, ______ _________?

2. You will get ____ ___________ from someone. __________ _________ _____ ________ _____ ____________ and decide_______ ________ _______ in it.

3. Next month _________ ________ ________ anywhere ______ __________ ______________ and take______________ with you. ____________ _________ _________ _________ and who __________ _______ ________ with you?

Discussion ❀

Discuss the three wishes with your partner. Compare your choices.

Follow-up activities ❀

1. With your partner, make up several more future wishes.
   Examples:
   a. Next week you will be given a car. What car will you choose?
   b. Someone will come tomorrow and paint both the inside and the outside of your house at no charge. However, it must all be in the same color, and it can't be white. Choose your color.

   Ask another group your questions, and answer their questions.

2. In three or four minutes tell your partner a fairy tale from your country.

International Adoptions

full text on page 113 (cd track 22)

Introduction ❀

In international adoptions, American couples or single people become the legal and permanent parents of children born in other countries. People who want to adopt must follow the rules of their country for legal adoption and the rules of the country where the child (usually a baby) was born. Nowadays, China, South Korea, Guatemala, and Ethiopia are examples of countries where Americans find children to adopt.

Vocabulary, Pronunciation ❀

1. **an adoption agency**: a business that helps people adopt
2. **a couple**: two people (in this lesson, a married couple)
3. **gender**: girl or boy; masculine or feminine
4. **permanent**: for a lifetime; forever
5. **a social worker**: a person who helps families with different problems

Pair Dictation ❀ Student A

Work in pairs and dictate to each other. Student A has half of the dictation and reads their lines to Student B, who has the other half. A dictates and B writes; then Student B dictates and A writes, until the dictation is complete. With your partner, correct the dictation.

When Americans (____________ ____ _______________) want a family _____

_______ _________ have a child ____ ____________ ______, they often decide

_____ _______________. Sometimes Americans ______ _____ __________

_____________to find a child. ________ ____________with adoption agencies.

_________________ _______________ _________ them with information _________

_____ ____________, such as age, health, _______ _____________. There are rules

_______________ _________ _____________. For example, Americans _________

____________ _____ country once or twice, _____ ________ ______ ___________

and the social workers. _________ _______ ______ _________ the child home.

The _________ _____ ________________ a child can be ____ ____ _____________.

Pair Dictation ❀ Student B

Work in pairs and dictate to each other. Student A has half of the dictation and reads their lines to Student B, who has the other half. A dictates and B writes; then Student B dictates and A writes, until the dictation is complete. With your partner, correct the dictation.

________ ____________________ (single or married) ________ __ __________

but they cannot__________ ____ ____________ of their own, _________

_________ ______________ to adopt. ______________ ______________ go to

other countries______ ___________ ____ ____________. They work ________

_____________ _____________. Adoption agencies help _________ _______

_________________ about the child, _______ _____ _________, ___________,

and gender. _________ ______ ____________ everyone must follow. ______

________________, __________________ must visit the _______________

__________ ___ _____________, and meet the child ______ _____ ____________

_____________. Then they can take ______ ____________ ___________. ____

cost of adopting ____ __________ ______ ______ up to $30,000.

Discussion ❀

Work with a partner and talk about your answers.

1. Why do people adopt a child?
2. How do adoption agencies help people who want to adopt?
3. Why do you think Americans often go to other countries to adopt?
4. Why, do you think, is it difficult to adopt a baby in the U.S.?
5. Is adoption acceptable in your culture?
6. How do you feel about adoption?
7. Why do people give up a child for adoption?
8. What problems do you see when someone adopts a child?
9. Do you think single people should adopt children?
10. What problems do you see with international adoptions?

Follow-up activity ❀

Think of some questions you would ask a single working woman or man who wants to adopt a baby. With a partner, perform a role play between the woman or man and a social worker.

Names

full text on page 113 (cd track 23)

Introduction ❀

A family name is also called a surname or a last name. It tells what family a person belongs to. In many European, North American, and South American cultures the family name is the last part of a person's name. In most countries in Asia, like China, Korea, Japan, and Vietnam, the family name comes first.

Vocabulary, Pronunciation ❀

1. **a nickname**: a silly name or a shortened form of someone's real name, usually given by friends or family
2. **a smith**: someone who makes and repairs things made of iron or other metal
3. **a surname**: family name

Pair Dictation ❀ Student A

Work in pairs and dictate to each other. Student A has half of the dictation and reads their lines to Student B, who has the other half. A dictates and B writes; then Student B dictates and A writes, until the dictation is complete. With your partner, correct the dictation.

There are ______________ __________ of American names. One kind

______ _______________ from jobs. ____________ ________ __________

popular names are __________, _________________, Smith, and Baker.

________ __________ is names __________ __________. It includes names

like ____________, __________, ______ _________.

We also get names __________ __________ ____________ family, __________

______________ (John's son).

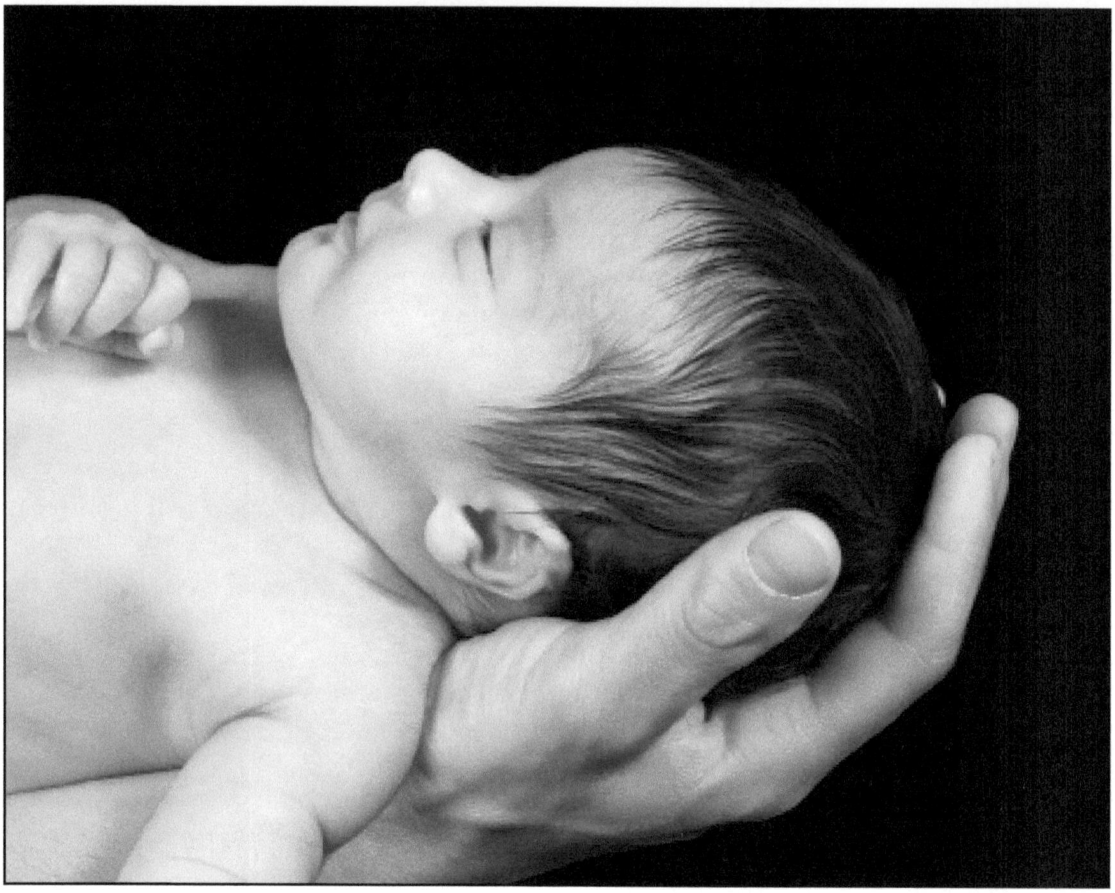

Pair Dictation ❀ Student B

Work in pairs and dictate to each other. Student A has half of the dictation and reads their lines to Student B, who has the other half. A dictates and B writes; then Student B dictates and A writes, until the dictation is complete. With your partner, correct the dictation.

________________ __________ several kinds _______ ________________

_________. _________ __________ is names _________ ______________.

Some of these ______________ ____________ ________ Cook, Carpenter,

____________, ________ ___________.

Another kind ________ ________ from colors. _____ ___________

_____________ _______ Brown, White, and Black.

______ ___________ _________ _____________ that are about ________,

like Johnson (__________ _____).

Discussion ❀

With a partner, discuss the following questions.

1. Tell your partner your full name (your first and last and any middle name). Talk about everything you know about your names. Do you know the meanings of the names? Are these popular names in your country? Were you named after anyone, such as a living or dead relative, or a famous person?

2. Many people who have come to the United States have changed their names. Sometimes they have changed their last names to make them shorter and also to sound more American. Others have taken different English first names because it was difficult for English-speaking people to pronounce their names. Have you or your family changed your names in any way? Would you?

3. Many women take their husband's name when they marry. If you're a woman, would you take your husband's name? If you're a man, would you expect your wife to take your name? What is done in your country when people marry?

4. Do you have a nickname that friends and family call you? What is it?

5. If you had twins, a boy and a girl, what would you name them? Why?

Follow-up activity ✣

Punctuation

The following paragraph is missing punctuation and capital letters. Put these in, and then take turns reading the paragraph aloud.

in the united states the family names of many african americans began in slavery many of them were given the surnames of their owners many freed slaves either created family names for themselves or took the names of their former owners others such as muhammad ali and malcolm x changed their names rather than live with the one the slave owner had given to their ancestors

Overweight

full text on page 114 (cd track 24)

Introduction ❀

Sixty-four percent (64%) of Americans are overweight and twenty-six point six percent (26.6%) are obese. What can the U.S. government do? In Japan the government did something about people who are overweight. The government calls this "metabo."

Vocabulary, Pronunciation ❀

1. **an inch**: 2.54 centimeters
2. **to measure**: to find the size, length, or amount of something
3. **obese**: very fat in a way that is not healthy
4. **overweight**: too heavy or too fat
5. **a pound**: 16 ounces or 0.454 kilograms
6. **a waist**: the part of your body just above your hips
7. **a waistline**: the area around your waist where you may wear a belt

Pair Dictation ❀ Student A

Work in pairs and dictate to each other. Student A has half of the dictation and reads their lines to Student B, who has the other half. A dictates and B writes; then Student B dictates and A writes, until the dictation is complete. With your partner, correct the dictation.

In 2008 _____ _____________ _____________ made _____ _____. It said

_______ _____________ and _____________ would measure _____ _____________

of all people _____________ _____ _____________ of 40 and 74. _____ ______

_____________ must be ______ _____________ or under. _____ ____________

_____________ must be ______ _____________ or under. _____ _____________

_____________ is too big, _____ _____ _____ to lose weight _____ ______

_____________ about nutrition and diet.

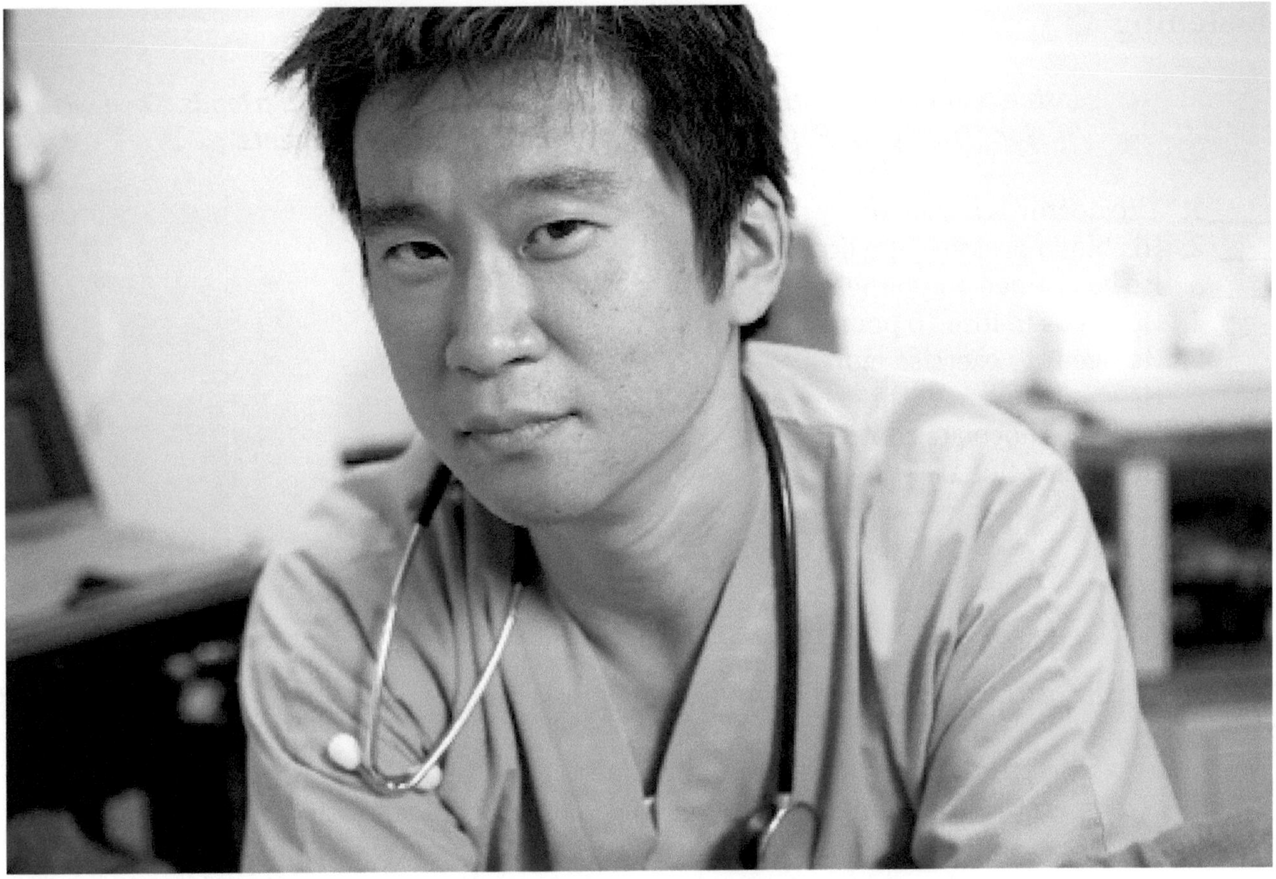

Japanese doctors take being overweight very seriously.

Pair Dictation ❀ Student B

Work in pairs and dictate to each other. Student A has half of the dictation and reads their lines to Student B, who has the other half. A dictates and B writes; then Student B dictates and A writes, until the dictation is complete. With your partner, correct the dictation.

_____ ____________ the Japanese government ____________ a law. ______ ________ that doctors ______ nurses __________ ____________ the waistlines _____ ______ ____________ between the ages ______ ______ ______ ______. A man's waistline ________ ______ 33.4 inches _____ ___________. A woman's waistline _______ ______ 35.4 inches ______ ___________. If someone's waistline ______ _______ _______, they must try _____ ________ ____________ or take classes _______ ________________ _____ __________.

Listening ❀

Listen to the conversation between Tom and George, two good friends. Then write "T" for "True" and "F" for "False" next to the following statements.

____ 1. The doctor is a woman.
____ 2. His blood pressure is a little low.
____ 3. He has gained 15 pounds.
____ 4. He needs to lose 10 pounds.
____ 5. He needs to exercise more.
____ 6. He should exercise three times a week.
____ 7. He likes chocolate cookies.
____ 8. He doesn't like salty foods.

Discussion ❀

With a partner, discuss the following questions.

1. The government is worried that that overweight people will have health problems. In Japan the government pays everyone's hospital bills, doctor bills, and medicines. The government is worried about older people's health and the higher medical costs for older people who are overweight.
   Who pays for hospitals, doctors, and medicine in your country?
2. Do you think you have good, average, or bad medical care in your country?
3. Should governments try to help people lose weight? What are some of the things governments can do?
4. What are some of the reasons people are getting fatter? (in the U.S., Europe, Japan)

Follow-up activity ❀

The U.S. Department of Agriculture has established a website called Mypyramid.gov to give people advice on healthy eating. The pyramid has six food groups with suggestions on what to eat. Their suggestions are below. Give yourself a test on your eating habits. Then write a "report card."

5 points: I do this a lot.
4 points: I do this often.
3 points: I do this sometimes.
2 points: I don't do this very much.
1 point: I rarely do this.

☛ GRAINS – ***"Make half your grains whole."***
- _____ Eat at least three ounces of whole grain bread, cereal, crackers, rice, or pasta every day.

☛ VEGETABLES – ***"Vary your veggies."***
- _____ Eat dark green veggies.
- _____ Eat orange veggies.
- _____ Eat dry beans and peas.

☛ FRUITS – ***"Focus on fruits."***
- _____ Eat a lot of fruits.
- _____ Eat a variety of fruits.
- _____ Go easy on fruit juice.

☛ MILK – ***"Get your calcium-rich foods."***
- _____ Go low-fat or fat-free.

☛ MEAT AND BEANS – ***"Go lean on protein."***
- _____ Choose low-fat or lean meat and poultry.
- _____ Bake, broil, or grill; don't fry.
- _____ Vary your choices with more fish, beans, peas, nuts, and seeds.

☛ OILS – ***"Know your fats."***
- _____ Make most of your fat sources from fish, nuts, and vegetable oils.
- _____ Limit solid fats like butter, stick margarine, shortening, and lard.

My Score _____

Adapted from "Inside the Pyramid" *in www.Mypyramid.gov*

Coffee, Coffee, and More Coffee

full text on page 115 (cd track 25)

Introduction ❀

Some people want to be the best at something or be the first to do something. Charles Lindbergh wanted to be the first to fly across the Atlantic Ocean. Sir Edmund Hilary wanted to be the first to climb Mt. Everest. This pair dictation is about a man who wanted to do something different.

Vocabulary, Pronunciation ❀

1. **caffeinated**: coffee with caffeine (a chemical that makes you feel more active)
2. **a computer programmer**: a person who programs computers
3. **decaffeinated coffee (decaf)**: coffee without caffeine
4. **Starbucks**: a popular chain of coffee shops
5. **2,468**: two thousand, four hundred and sixty-eight
6. **8,971**: eight thousand, nine hundred and seventy-one
7. **11,439**: eleven thousand, four hundred and thirty-nine

Pair Dictation ❀ Student A

Work in pairs and dictate to each other. Student A has half of the dictation and reads to Student B, who has the other half. A dictates and B writes; then Student B dictates and A writes, until the dictation is complete. With your partner, correct the dictation.

John "Winter" Smith, ___ ____- ______-_____ computer programmer, _________ _____ _________ coffee in every Starbucks ___ _____ __________. He started to do this _____ ______. By 2013 he had ________ _______ ______ ________ of decaffeinated coffee _____ _____________ ____________ _______ North America, ________ ____________ _______________around the world.____________ __________ _____ __________________28 shops ________ _________ ______________ city.

When he gets ________ __________ __________, he drinks ________ _____________, takes a ___________ of the shop, ______ ____________. He is not _________ ________ ___________ _______________ you often see ______ _____________ reading books _______ _______________ _______ ______________ computers.

Pair Dictation ❀ Student B

Work in pairs and dictate to each other. Student A has half of the dictation and reads to Student B, who has the other half. A dictates and B writes; then Student B dictates and A writes, until the dictation is complete. With your partner, correct the dictation.

__________ "__________" __________, a 42-year-old __________ __________, wants to drink __________ ______ __________ __________ in the world. __________ __________ ______ ______ __________ in 1997. ______ __________ ______ __________ drunk half a cup______ __________ __________ in 8,971 Starbucks in __________ __________ __________, and 2, 468 Starbucks __________ ______ __________. One day he visited __________ __________ in one American __________.

__________ ______ __________ to a shop, ______ __________ his coffee, __________ ______ picture ______ __________ ______ and leaves. ______ ______ ______ one of the people __________ __________ __________ at Starbucks __________ __________ or working on their __________.

Discussion ❀

The question many people ask "Winter" is "Why are you doing this?" His answer is that he likes to collect things. He collects comic books, cards, and coins. He says that once he begins, he has to get all of them. It is the same for Starbucks. He has to collect them all.

With a partner, discuss the following questions.

1. People collect all kinds of things – comic books, baseball cards, Barbie dolls. Why do you think people like to collect things?
2. Have you ever collected anything? Tell us about it.
3. We don't know a lot about "Winter." Imagine him. Is he married? Does he have children? What does he look like? Do you think he is a strange man?
4. Are you a coffee drinker? How much do you drink every day?
5. Do you ever drink decaf? Why?
6. Do you ever drink caffe latte, espresso, or cappuccino? Do you have a favorite coffee drink?
7. Slang expressions for coffee in the U.S. are java and Joe. Do you know of any others? What is the word for coffee in your country?

Follow-up activity ❀

1. **Use the Web**

   Go to Winter's website, **StarbucksEverywhere.net** or his blog or his journal. What did you learn about him? Present this information to the class.

   Winter has pictures of every Starbucks he has visited. Has he visited your city? Was there a picture of a Starbucks you have visited?

   As of June 2013, Winter had visited 11,439 Starbucks. Some of the countries he has visited are China, Taiwan, Turkey, and Mexico. What are two other countries he visited?

2. **Listening to, Reading, and Writing Large Numbers**

   If you have three numbers, you read it as hundreds.
   114 = one hundred and fourteen
   If you have four, five, or six numbers, you read it as thousands.
   4,122 = four thousand one hundred and twenty-two
   41,220 = forty-one thousand, two hundred and twenty
   410,220 = four hundred and ten thousand, two hundred and twenty

   Now it's your turn. Write down four numbers. Be sure you know how to say them. Now read them to your partner, who will write them down. Your partner will read their numbers to you.

Intermarriage

full text on page 116 (cd track 26)

Introduction ❀

In the early days of U.S. history, most "Americans" were either Europeans, Native Indians, or, in the Southwest, Hispanic people. Slavery brought Africans to America in 1619. In the 1900s many more immigrants came from Europe. And in recent years Asians and Latinos have become a large part of the American population. Today, intermarriage among Americans from different heritages is changing the face of the "Average American."

Vocabulary, Pronunciation ❀

1. **Hispanic**: Spanish-speaking
2. **slavery**: a practice of owning human beings
3. **a Latino**: a person having roots in Latin America
4. **a heritage**: a cultural background and tradition

Pair Dictation ❀ Student A

Work in pairs and dictate to each other. Student A has half of the dictation and reads their lines to Student B, who has the other half. A dictates and B writes; then Student B dictates and A writes, until the dictation is complete. With your partner, correct the dictation.

One hundred _______ ____, most immigrants _______ ____ ____________ from Europe. _______ _________________ ________ to school _______ ____-_______________ American children. When the new Americans ______________, they often ___________ _________________ from other heritages.

Today, the same is true _____ __________-___________________ and Latinos. ________ _______ ___________ non-Asians and non-Latinos. _____ ___________, about one-half of Asian women __________ _____-_______ _______. About one-third of ____-________ __________ marry non-Latinos.

Pair Dictation ❀ Student B

Work in pairs and dictate to each other. Student A has half of the dictation and reads their lines to Student B, who has the other half. A dictates and B writes; then Student B dictates and A writes, until the dictation is complete. With your partner, correct the dictation.

______ ____________ years ago, _______ ___________________ came to America _____ ______________. Their children went ____ ______________ with non-immigrant ____________ ___________. _______ ______ _______ ______________ married, _____ ________ married Americans ______ _______ __________________.

________, _____ _______ ____ _________ for Asian-Americans _____ ___________. They often marry ____-_________ _____ _____-_________. For example, ______ _____-_______ ____ ________ ___________ marry non-Asian men. _______ _____-_________ ____ U.S.-born Latinos __________ ____-___________.

Discussion ❀

Work with a partner and answer these questions. Share your responses with the class.

1. Why do you think people choose to intermarry?
2. Are you surprised by the percentages of intermarriage among the different groups? Is there much intermarriage in your country among people of different heritages?
3. The majority of Latinos in the U.S. are from Mexico. Why?
4. What do you know about the Asian-American population?

Follow-up activity ❀

Write a paragraph about this couple.
Who are they? Where do they live?
How old are they? What are their jobs?
Where and when are they getting married?

A Historic Day

full text on page 117 (cd track 27)

Introduction ❀

On November 4, 2008, Americans elected the first black president of the United States, Barack Obama. He comes from Chicago, Illinois, but his early life experiences are quite different from those of other politicians. What do you know about him? Here is a short biography.

Work with a partner and read the sentences, which outline a short biography of Barack Obama. Put them in chronological or logical order.

____ His father, from Kenya, met his mother, from Hawaii, at the University of Hawaii in Manoa in the early '60s. They divorced in 1964.

____ Obama taught Constitutional Law at the University of Chicago Law School from 1992 to 2002.

____ Obama attended schools in Jakarta, Indonesia, until he was ten years old. His mother had married an Indonesian and lived there off and on for years.

__1__ Barack Obama was born on August 4, 1961, in Hawaii.

____ He graduated from Columbia University in 1983 and from Harvard Law in 1991.

____ When he left Indonesia he went to live with his maternal grandparents in Honolulu.

____ He became a U.S. Senator from Illinois in 2004 with 70% of the vote.

____ He married Michelle Robinson in 1992. They have two daughters, Malia and Sasha.

____ After graduation from Columbia in 1983, he spent the next eight years working for various community service organizations. He later concentrated his law efforts on civil rights.

____ In 2012, Obama was re-elected U.S. President.

Vocabulary, Pronunciation ❀

1. **fully**: completely
2. **kids**: children
3. **Martin Luther King, Jr.**: a famous black American leader (1929–1968)
4. **a speech**: a talk
5. **truly**: really
6. **look *my son* in the eye**: be honest with *my son*

Pair Dictation ❀ Student A

Work in pairs and dictate to each other. Student A has half of the dictation and reads their lines to Student B, who has the other half. A dictates and B writes; then Student B dictates and A writes, until the dictation is complete. With your partner, correct the dictation.

Here are some comments from Americans, both black and white, when they learned that the United States would have its first African-American President.

1. **James Carson, 64**: I am surprised ______ ______________. I didn't ________ a black man ______________ _____ __________________ in my lifetime. _______ ____ ________ a child, _____________ _____________ couldn't even ____ ____ _____ same schools _____ _______________ – before 1965.

2. **LaToya Williams, 61**: Martin Luther King, Jr.'s _____________ ___________, "I have a dream,"_____ ________ ________ ______ _______. Obama will ____ President ______ ______ Americans, black ______ ______________.

3. **George Miller, 44**: ________ _____ _________ look my son ___ _____ ______ and say, "______ _________ _________ _____ whatever _______ ________to be, _______ ____ _____ ______________. I finally feel ________ ____________.

Pair Dictation ❀ Student B

Work in pairs and dictate to each other. Student A has half of the dictation and reads their lines to Student B, who has the other half. A dictates and B writes; then Student B dictates and A writes, until the dictation is complete. With your partner, correct the dictation.

Here are some comments from Americans, both black and white, when they learned that the United States would have its first African-American President.

1. **James Carson, 64**: ___ ________ ______________________ and happy. ___ ____________ think ____ ______________ _______ would be President ____ _____ _________________. When I was ____ ______________, black kids _____________ ________ go to the ________ _______________ as whites – ______________ __________.

2. **LaToya Williams, 61**: _____________ ____________ ___________, Jr.'s famous speech, "____ _________ ____ ___________," is now true for us. ___________ _____ be ________________ for all ________________, _____________ and white.

3. **George Miller, 44**: Now I can ________ ______ _______ in the eye ______ ________," You can truly be _____________ you want ____ ____, even a U.S. President. ___ ____________ _______ fully American.

Discussion ❀

With a partner, discuss the following questions.

1. Does your country have national elections? How do you choose your leaders?
2. Does your country ever have minority leaders?
3. Is Obama's election important for the U.S.? Explain.

Follow-up activity ❀

1. *Do a search to discover how many states voted for Obama in both the 2008 and 2012 elections. Report back to the class.*
2. *What is Obamacare? Medicare?*

Medical Myths

full text on page 118 (cd track 28)

Introduction ❀

People in some countries think that if you know what someone's blood type is (A, AB, B, O) you will have some idea of what a person is like. For example, they believe that if you are Type A you are serious and creative, but overanxious. There are no scientific studies for this belief. This is a medical myth. Do you know of any other medical myths?

Vocabulary, Pronunciation ❀

1. **a blood type**: human blood can be classified into types
2. **creative**: being able to produce new ideas, make new things like art
3. **dim**: not bright
4. **a myth**: an idea or story that many people believe, but that is not true
5. **overanxious**: too worried about many things that may or may not happen

Pair Dictation ❀ Student A

Work in pairs and dictate to each other. Student A has half of the dictation and reads their lines to Student B, who has the other half. A dictates and B writes; then Student B dictates and A writes, until the dictation is complete. With your partner, correct the dictation.

Our parents _______ _____________ told us _______ _____________

in dim light ____________ hurt _________ ___________. But most eye

doctors _______ _______ ____________ in low light ________

not hurt _______ ________.

There are ___________ _____________ _________ that people believe

__________ ______ ______ ___________. For example, ________ ______

________________ do not continue ____ ____________ after someone dies.

________, _____________ ________ does not make it _______ ________ faster

and darker.

Pair Dictation ❀ Student B

Work in pairs and dictate to each other. Student A has half of the dictation and reads their lines to Student B, who has the other half. A dictates and B writes; then Student B dictates and A writes, until the dictation is complete. With your partner, correct the dictation.

_______ _____________ and teachers ___________ _____ that reading

_____ ________ ___________ will __________ our eyes. ______ _________

_______ ____________ say that reading _____ _______ __________ does

_____ _________ our eyes.

_____________ ______ other medical myths ________ ____________

_____________ which are not true. ______ ___________, hair and fingernails

______ _______ _________________ to grow _______ ______________

__________. Also, shaving hair ______ _______ ____________ _____ grow

back ___________ _______ ______________.

Discussion ❀

1. *With a partner, discuss the following question.*

   Did you or do you believe any of the myths mentioned in this unit? (blood types, reading in low light, fingernails and hair, shaving and hair)

2. *With a partner, discuss and decide if the following are true (T) or False (F). Your teacher will give you the answers when you're finished.*

a. ______ It is healthier to have lower blood pressure than higher blood pressure.
b. ______ We should drink eight glasses of water every day.
c. ______ Eating turkey can make people sleepy.
d. ______ By 50, the average person's hair is about half gray, white, or silver.
e. ______ We use only 10% of our brains.
f. ______ Generally women live longer than men.
g. ______ Gray hair is caused by stress.

Follow-up activity ❀

Ask five people outside the class if they believe in the four myths from the dictation: Blood types, Dim light, After death growth, Shaving hair. Report back to the class.

Ken's Cadillacs

full text on page 119 (cd track 29)

Introduction ❀

Sometimes we accidentally dial the wrong number. What do you do or say when you discover you've made a mistake? Or when someone calls ***you*** by mistake?

Vocabulary, Pronunciation ❀

1. **a Cadillac**: an American car
2. **a dealership**: a place to buy a car
3. **a steakhouse**: a restaurant where you can get steak
4. **tense**: nervous

Pair Dictation ❀ Student A

Work in pairs and dictate to each other. Student A has half of the dictation and reads their lines to Student B, who has the other half. A dictates and B writes; then Student B dictates and A writes, until the dictation is complete. With your partner, correct the dictation.

"Ken's, good morning," ______ ____________ ______________ said when he ____________ _____ __________ at his car ______________, Ken's Cadillacs. _______ ___________ asked about _______ ________, and my brother ___________ that they opened ____ ________ ______ closed between _________ ______ ______ ______.

"You're saying _________ ___________ for lunch? But _________ ___________ _________," the woman said.

"Well, ______ ________ _______," Ken ___________.

The conversation ______ ________ ________ tense until they ______________ _______ the woman had _____ __________ _____________. She had been __________ _____ reach Ken's ______________!

Pair Dictation ❀ Student B

Work in pairs and dictate to each other. Student A has half of the dictation and reads their lines to Student B, who has the other half. A dictates and B writes; then Student B dictates and A writes, until the dictation is complete. With your partner, correct the dictation.

"__________, ___________ ________________," my brother Ken _________ ___________ ______ answered the phone _____ ________ ________ dealership, _________ __________________. The caller ________ __________ their hours, ______ _____ ____________ explained _______ ________ _____________ at 9 but __________ ______________ 12 and 1 p.m.

"____________ _________ you're closed ______ __________? ______ that's really crazy," _______ ______________ _________.

"_________, we gotta eat," _________ said.

______ ___________________ got even more ____________ ___________ __________ realized that ______ _______________ _____ the wrong number. ______ _______ ________ trying to ___________ _______ Steakhouse!

Comprehension Questions

With a partner, answer the following questions.

1. What was the name of the car dealership?
2. What time did the dealership close for lunch?
3. Why was the woman surprised when they said they closed for lunch?
4. What business was she trying to call?

Discussion

1. *Work with a partner and see how many you can name.*

   a. How many American cars can you name? ***Example:*** Cadillac
   b. How many Japanese cars can you name?
   c. How many German cars can you name?

2. *With a partner, decide what business you might be calling. More than one answer is possible. Share your answers with the class.*

   Example: **HAPPY SMILES** – a dentist's office, a circus, a fun park

   a. **BOB'S AUTO BODY**
   b. **THE DOG HOUSE**
   c. **THE RIGHT CUT**
   d. **COOL IT**
   e. **GRANDMOTHER'S ATTIC**
   f. **SWEET PLEASURES**
   g. **BATH AND BODY WORKS**

Follow-up activities

1. *Think of a joke and tell it to the class.*
2. *Tell the class about an experience you had when you called the wrong number or when someone mistakenly called you.*

The Top Three

full text on page 120 (cd track 30)

Introduction ❀

Here's a fun activity. Guess the top three answers!

Vocabulary, Pronunciation ❀

1. **oatmeal**: a cooked breakfast food made from oats
2. **lipstick**: an oil-based cosmetic for coloring the lips
3. **a stew**: A slow-cooked thick soup with beef or chicken
4. **to inherit**: to receive money or property, mainly from a deceased family member

Pair Dictation ❀ Student A

In this dictation, work in pairs and dictate to each other. Student A has half of the sentence and reads their lines to Student B, who has the other half (A dictates and B writes). Then Student B dictates and A writes until the sentence is complete. When you are finished, check your sentences with your partner. ***After the dictation, work with your partner and choose/guess the top three responses from an informal American survey.***

1. What's a good food _____ ________ _____ _______ on a cold night?
   a. hot chocolate b. oatmeal c. soup d. stew e. chili f. pizza

2. __________ ______ _____ _________ to get rich quick?
   a. inherit it b. steal it c. marry money d. win the lottery
   e. gamble f. invest in good stocks

3. Name a way ____ __________ _________________ in another language.
   a. ciao b. adios c. sayonara d. au revoir e. zai jan f. dasvidaniya

4. _______ ______________ ______________ do girls start wearing lipstick?
   a. 12 b. 13 c. 14 d. 15 e. 16 f. 11

5. Name a favorite ______________ _________________ _________.
   a. Florida b. Las Vegas c. Puerto Rico d. Disneyland
   e. New York City f. Bahamas

6. What is something people do __________ __________ __________________?
   a. pay taxes b. vote c. serve in the military d. be a politician
   e. work for the government

7. ________ ____ ____________ that is always in demand.
a. soldier b. nurse c. doctor d. fireman e. policeman f. teacher

8. Name a holiday ________ ______ ______ ______________.
a. New Year's Eve b. Memorial Day c. July 4th d. Thanksgiving
e. Columbus Day f. Veterans Day

Pair Dictation ❀ Student B

In this dictation, work in pairs and dictate to each other. Student A has half of the sentence and reads their lines to Student B, who has the other half (A dictates and B writes). Then Student B dictates and A writes until the sentence is complete. When you are finished, check your sentences with your partner. ***After the dictation, work with your partner and choose/guess the top three responses from an informal American survey.***

1. ______ ____ ________ ________ that warms you up __ __ ____ ______?
a. hot chocolate b. oatmeal c. soup d. stew e. chili f. pizza

2. What is a way____ _______ _________ __________?
a. inherit it b. steal it c. marry money d. win the lottery
e. gamble f. invest in good stocks

3. ________ ____ ________ to say goodbye ___ __________
__________.
a. ciao b. adios c. sayonara d. au revoir e. zai jan f. dasvidaniya

4. At what age _____ _________ _________ _________
__________?
a. 12 b. 13 c. 14 d. 15 e. 16 f. 11

5. _________ _____ ____________ American vacation spot.
a. Florida b. Las Vegas c. Puerto Rico d. Disneyland
e. New York City f. Bahamas

6. ______ ____ __________ __________ _____ for their country?
a. pay taxes b. vote c. serve in the military d. be a politician
e. work for the government

7. Name an occupation ________ ____ ____________ ____ __________.
a. soldier b. nurse c. doctor d. fireman e. policeman f. teacher

8. ________ __ ____________ that can be dangerous.
a. New Year's Eve b. Memorial Day c. July 4th d. Thanksgiving
e. Columbus Day f. Veterans Day

Discussion ❀

With a partner, choose one or more answers. Compare it with your classmates.

1. Name an animal that is black and white.
2. Name a dangerous job.
3. Name a part of the body mentioned in love songs.
4. What is something people add sugar to?
5. What do bees do?
6. Name a fruit that is the size of a tennis ball.
7. Name the heaviest thing in your apartment/house.
8. Name an age that's good to marry.
9. What is a color you wouldn't paint your house?
10. Name something a woman might have in her medicine cabinet.
11. Name an animal that could swallow you.
12. Name someone or something that starts with the word "lady."

Discussion ❀

Work with a partner and decide if the following statements are "fact" or "opinion."

___ 1. Barack Obama was the first African -American U.S. President.

___ 2. Barack Obama was the best U.S. President.

___ 3. A U.S. president makes $400,000 a year.

___ 4. $60,000 is a pretty good salary for an experienced teacher.

___ 5. Teachers need four years of university to qualify for teaching.

___ 6. Most present-day U.S. presidents have law degrees.

___ 7. Most politicians are dishonest.

Follow-up Activities ❀ *Choose one.*

1. Watch the TV program, *Family Feud*. Write down some questions and answers you can share with your classmates.
2. Write a short paragraph on "What I Can Do for My Country."

School Uniforms

full text on page 121 (cd track 31)

Introduction ❀

In most public elementary, middle, junior high, and high schools in the United States, students do not wear uniforms. Students in some private and some religious private schools wear uniforms, but in others they don't. What do you think are the advantages and disadvantages of having to wear a school uniform?

Vocabulary, Pronunciation ❀

1. **baggy pants**: pants that are too big and look as if they are falling down
2. **a blazer**: a formal jacket often worn with slacks or a skirt, instead of a suit
3. **denim**: cloth, usually blue, that jeans are made of
4. **flip-flops**: very light slipper-like or beach-like shoes
5. **hoodies**: soft jackets with zippers and head covering

Pair Dictation ❀ Student A

Work in pairs and dictate to each other. Student A has half of the dictation and reads to Student B, who has the other half. A dictates and B writes; then Student B dictates and A writes, until the dictation is complete. With your partner, correct the dictation.

When you went ______ ______________, did you ever ____________ _____
____________________? If you didn't wear one, __________ _______________
____________ ______________ about what you could wear ________ __________
________ ________________ ___________? In most public schools _____ ________
_______________ _______________ there are no uniforms. However, in some towns and cities _______________ _____ __________ ______________ you can't wear
______ ______________. Some examples of these __________ _______________
-______________, ____________________, and baggy pants _______________
____________ __________.

Students often disagree _______________ _______________ _______________. They say, "People _______________ _______________ __________ ___________ they want to dress. _______ _________ ___ _______________ _______ the way I express myself."

Pair Dictation ❀ Student B

Work in pairs and dictate to each other. Student A has half of the dictation and reads to Student B, who has the other half; A dictates and B writes; then Student B dictates and A writes, until the dictation is complete. With your partner, correct the dictation.

__________ __________ __________ to school, __________ __________
__________ wear a uniform? __________ __________ __________
__________ __________, were there any rules __________ __________
__________ __________ __________ and what you couldn't wear?
__________ __________ __________ __________ in the
United States __________ __________ __________ __________.
__________, _____ __________ __________ __________
__________ there are some things __________ __________
__________ to school. __________ __________ _____
__________ are flip-flops, hoodies, __________ __________
__________ pulled down low.

__________ __________ __________ with these rules. __________
__________, "__________ should dress the way __________
__________ _____ __________. The way I dress is __________
__________ __ __________ __________."

Listening ❀

Listen to the conversation between two friends. Then check off (✓) any item of clothing you hear in the conversation.

baggy pants	hoodies	shirts
baseball Caps	jeans	skirts
dresses	knee socks	socks
earrings	maxi skirts	tee shirts
flip-flops	mini skirts	ties
tights	white shirts	

Discussion ❀ *With a partner, discuss the following questions.*

Did you wear a uniform to school? Tell your partner about it and describe it.

What do you think are the advantages and disadvantages of school uniforms?

Have you ever worn a uniform? In the military? In an organization like Boy Scouts or Girl Scouts?

Do you agree that "The way I dress is the way I express myself"?

Do you often judge people by the way they dress?

Follow-up activities ❀

Do one of the following activities.

1. Bring a picture or draw a picture of yourself in a uniform. Show it to the class and talk about it.
2. Write about a time you had to wear a school, military, or organization uniform.
3. Draw a picture of someone wearing at least five items of clothing mentioned in this chapter. Label the items of clothing.

Rosa Parks

full text on page 122 (cd track 32)

Introduction ✤

Before the 1960s in the segregated South, African-Americans could not attend the same universities as whites, stay at the same hotels as whites, or use the same restrooms or swimming pools as whites. Rosa Parks, 42, an African-American, was tired of living in a segregated society, so when she sat in the blacks-only section of the city bus one day in December 1955, she made an important decision. Here is her story.

Vocabulary, Pronunciation ✤

1. **to boycott**: in this case: to stop riding the buses because of unfair laws
2. **filled up**: got crowded
3. **a jail**: a prison
4. **Negroes**: another word for blacks or African-Americans, used before the 1960s
5. **a seat**: a place to sit on a bus
6. **segregated**: separated

Prediction ✤ *In this dictation you are not going to listen first. Work with a partner and fill in each blank with a word you think is correct. When you are finished, listen, and do the dictation on the next page. Then compare your answers.*

Every day for years, Rosa Parks got on ________ bus to go to work in Montgomery, Alabama. __________ always sat in the first row of the black section at the back of the _________. Whites sat _________ the front section. One morning as Rosa was going _______ work, the bus filled up with both whites ________ blacks. The bus driver shouted to the Negroes to give up _____________ seats to the whites. Rosa did not move. She stayed in her _____________ and looked out the window. She was tired of ___________ telling her what to do. The bus driver __________ angry and called the police. The police came and took _________ to jail. When the black community ______________ that Rosa was in jail, they decided to take action. With the help _____ Dr. Martin Luther King, Jr., the blacks in the ____________ organized a bus boycott. 95% of the blacks in the city stopped ____________ the buses to and from work. The boycott lasted 381 days. Finally, _______Supreme Court declared segregation on buses unconstitutional. Rosa had started ________ important revolution.

Rosa Parks and Martin Luther King, Jr.

Dictation ✣ *Listen and fill in the blanks with the words you hear. Then, with a partner, compare your prediction to the dictation.*

Every day for years, Rosa Parks got on ________ bus to go to work in Montgomery, Alabama. __________ always sat in the first row of the black section at the back of the_________. Whites sat ______ the front section. One morning as Rosa was going _______ work, the bus filled up with both whites ________ blacks. The bus driver shouted to the Negroes to give up _____________seats to the whites. Rosa did not move. She stayed in her _____________ and looked out the window. She was tired of ___________ telling her what to do. The bus driver __________ angry and called the police. The police came and took _________ to jail. When the black community ______________ that Rosa was in jail, they decided to take action. With the help _____ Dr. Martin Luther King, Jr., the blacks in the ____________ organized a bus boycott. 95% of the blacks in the city stopped ____________ the buses to and from work. The boycott lasted 381 days. Finally, _______ Supreme Court declared segregation on buses unconstitutional. Rosa had started ________ important revolution.

Discussion ✤

1. *Work with a partner and decide who spoke these words.*

   a. ________________ "Negroes! Get up and give your seats to the whites."

   b. ________________ "We will help change this unfair law and organize a boycott."

   c. ________________ "I never allowed myself to be treated as a second-class citizen. You must respect yourself before others can respect you."

   d. ________________ "I did not feel I was breaking the law, because I was not sitting in the front of the bus."

   e. ________________ "We now declare that segregation on Montgomery buses is unconstitutional."

2. *Here are some questions about the dictation.*

   a. How long ago did Rosa start an important revolution?
   b. Why did she take the bus every day?
   c. Why didn't she move from her seat?
   d. What did the bus driver do?
   e. What did the blacks in Montgomery do?
   f. Who helped them organize a boycott?
   g. Was the boycott successful? How?
   h. Why was this an important event for black Americans?

3. *Here are some important dates in black history. Ask your classmates questions about them.*
   Example: "When did slavery end?"

   1865 Slavery ended
   1956 Segregation on buses ended
   1963 Blacks entered the same universities as whites for the first time
   1968 Most segregated schools, hotels, and restaurants desegregated
   1968 Dr. King was assassinated
   2009 The first black American president was inaugurated

4. In the U.S. some groups of Americans are different from the majority of the people racially or culturally. They are called minorities. Does the country your family comes from have minorities? Are they segregated? Are they treated the same way as the majority?

Follow-up activity ✤ *Here are some other famous African-American women in U.S. history. Choose one and write a short biography of her life.*

Harriet Tubman	Jane Pittman	Sojourner Truth
Toni Morrison	Alice Walker	Maya Angelou

Asking For Advice

full text on page 123 (cd track 33)

Introduction ✣

Parents love their children and they want a good future for them. Parents and children often disagree about what to do in the future. Does this ever happen in your family?

Vocabulary, Pronunciation ✣

1. **advice**: opinion you give to someone about what to do
2. **to agree**: to have the same opinion or idea
3. **to disagree**: to have a different opinion

Prediction ✣ *In this dictation you are not going to listen first. Work with a partner and fill in each blank with a word you think is correct. When you are finished, listen and do the dictation on the next page. Then compare your answers.*

Dear Sandy,

I have ____ problem. I want ____ be a rock musician when I finish high school, but ____ father ________, "No!" I play the guitar _______ a group of friends after school, and we are _________to play for a big party _____our town next week. I can sing pretty _______, too. My father says, "Go to college and _________ business so you ______help us with our family's furniture business." Sometimes I _________ in the store on weekends, but it's boring. I don't ________ ____ go to college. My father is not a college graduate, so ________ is important to him. All I want to do is _______ the guitar and sing with my___________. What can I do?

Johnny Jagger

Comprehension Questions ✣ *With a partner, answer the following questions.*

1. What does Johnny want to be?
2. What instrument does he play?
3. What does his father want him to do? Why?
4. Is his father a college graduate?
5. About how old is Johnny?
6. What is your advice for Johnny?

Dictation ✣ *Listen and fill in the blanks with the words you hear. Then, with a partner, compare your prediction to the listening.*

Dear Sandy,

I have ____ problem. I want ____ be a rock musician when I finish high school, but ____ father ________, "No!" I play the guitar _______ a group of friends after school, and we are _________to play for a big party _____our town next week. I can sing pretty _______, too. My father says, "Go to college and _________ business so you ______help us with our family's furniture business." Sometimes I _________ in the store on weekends, but it's boring. I don't ________ ____ go to college. My father is not a college graduate, so ________ is important to him. All I want to do is _______ the guitar and sing with my___________. What can I do?

Johnny Jagger

Discussion or role play ✣ *Talk about the following situations.*

1. Susan is a high school senior; Bob is 26 and working as a hotel clerk. They say they love each other very much. Susan's parents think Bob is too old for her. They want her to go to college and get a good job before she gets married. What advice do you have for Susan?

2. Sarah is very intelligent and wants to go to a famous private college that is very expensive ($50,000 a year). Her parents do not make a lot of money. Sarah says she can work in a restaurant on weekends and during the summer. What advice do you have for Sarah?

Follow-up activity ✣ *Write a letter to Johnny, Susan, or Sarah and give them some advice.*

Fact or Opinion?

full text on page 123 (cd track 34)

Introduction ✣

A fact is a generally accepted statement of truth that can be checked in a dictionary, encyclopedia, or other reference source. An opinion, on the other hand, expresses a personal feeling, idea, or point of view. Here are some statements. Some are facts and some are opinions. Try them!

Vocabulary, Pronunciation ✣

1. **a disease**: an illness
2. **cancer**: a dangerous disease
3. **elected**: chosen by the people
4. **Haiti**: a country in the Caribbean Sea
5. **Morocco**: a country in northwestern Africa

Prediction ✣ *In this dictation you are not going to listen first. Work by yourself or with a partner and fill in each blank with a word you think is correct. When you are finished, listen and do the dictation on the next page. Then compare your answers. Remember to add the F for Fact and O for Opinion. The first one is done for you.*

_F_ 1. The Pacific Ocean is _the_ largest of the four oceans.

___ 2. The oldest university in the world _____ in Morocco.

___ 3. Chinese ____ more difficult to learn than Arabic.

___ 4. Paris is the most beautiful _______________ in Europe.

___ 5. A Honda Civic is less expensive______________ a Honda Accord.

___ 6. Democracy is the best form _____ government.

___ 7. Haiti is the poorest _________________ in the Western Hemisphere.

___ 8. History is more ____________________ than science.

___ 9. Cancer is the worst __________________ that a person can have.

___ 10. John F. Kennedy ________ the youngest man ever elected President ____ ______ United States.

Dictation ✣ *Listen and fill in the blanks with the words you hear. Then, with a partner, compare your prediction to the listening.*

F 1. The Pacific Ocean is the largest of the four oceans.

___ 2. The oldest university in the world _____ in Morocco.

___ 3. Chinese ____ more difficult to learn than Arabic.

___ 4. Paris is the most beautiful ______________ in Europe.

___ 5. A Honda Civic is less expensive______________ a Honda Accord.

___ 6. Democracy is the best form _____ government.

___ 7. Haiti is the poorest _________________ in the Western Hemisphere.

___ 8. History is more _____________________ than science.

___ 9. Cancer is the worst __________________ that a person can have.

___ 10. John F. Kennedy ________ the youngest man ever elected President ____ ______ United States.

Discussion ✣

With a partner, discuss the following questions. Then share your answers with the class.

1. Look at the "opinion" statements above. Do you agree or disagree with them? If you disagree, give your opinion, if you have one.
2. Give two statements about your home city and/or country. One must be a fact and one must be an opinion. See if your partner can guess which is which.

Follow-up activity ✣

Find out more information about a U.S. president. Write eight statements. Six of them must be factual and two of them opinion. Share your statements with the class.

Giant Pandas

full text on page 124 (cd track 35)

Introduction ✣

In zoos all over the world, one of the most popular animals is the giant panda. The pandas come from China and could become extinct if the area where they live (their habitat) changes, and the bamboo that they eat disappears. Some zoos have become successful at breeding pandas; several zoos now have baby pandas.

Vocabulary, Pronunciation ✣

1. **bamboo**: a tall tropical plant with green leaves; its stems are often used to make furniture.
2. **a cub**: a baby animal like a panda, a bear, a tiger, a lion
3. **extinct**: when all the animals of one kind are gone; it doesn't exist any more
4. **habitat**: a place where plants and animals grow and live. A forest is a kind of habitat.
5. **survive**: continue to live

Prediction ✣

In this dictation you are not going to listen first. Work with a partner and fill in each blank with a word you think is correct. When you are finished, listen and do the dictation on the next page. Then compare your answers.

Visitors to zoos think that giant ______________ __________ very cute, especially baby ______________. Pandas ______________ fur which is black and white. They are about three ______________ tall (91 centimeters) when they are standing on their four ______________.

Males weigh up to 250 ______________ (110 kilograms). ____________________ usually weigh less than 220 ______________ (100 __________________).

Pandas __________ as much as 40 pounds (18________________) of bamboo every __________. They spend ten to sixteen ____________ every __________ looking for ______________ and eating it. In zoos ______________ pandas eat some vegetables and fruit as well as ______________.

The female ____________ is ready to mate only once a ______________ for ________ or three days in the spring. She will have one or ____________ cubs. Often only __________ will survive.

Dictation ✣ *Listen and fill in the blanks with the words you hear. Then with a partner, compare your prediction to the listening.*

Visitors to zoos think that giant _____________ _________ very cute, especially baby ______________. Pandas _____________ fur which is black and white. They are about three _____________ tall (91 centimeters) when they are standing on their four _____________.

Males weigh up to 250 _____________ (110 kilograms). _________________ usually weigh less than 220 _____________ (100 ________________).

Pandas _________ as much as 40 pounds (18_______________) of bamboo every _________. They spend ten to sixteen ___________ every _________ looking for _____________ and eating it. In zoos _____________ pandas eat some vegetables and fruit as well as _____________.

The female ___________ is ready to mate only once a ____________ for _______ or three days in the spring. She will have one or ___________ cubs. Often only __________ will survive.

Discussion ✣

With a partner, discuss the following questions.

1. Have you ever seen a giant panda? Where?
2. Is it important to not let an animal become extinct? Do you know any other animals or plants that might become extinct?
3. Should we mate wild pandas in zoos? The babies will then spend the rest of their lives in zoos.

Follow-up activities ✣

1. *Learn more about the giant pandas. Go to the web or to a book. Present your information to the class.*
2. *Make a list of five other animals that might become extinct. Present your list to the class.*

A giant panda eating bamboo.

American Families

full text on page 125 (cd track 36)

Introduction ✣

Here are some interesting facts about American families today from the Council on Contemporary Families. Some of them will surprise you! For example: it is true that the fastest growing group of new members of Internet dating websites is people 50 years and older.

Vocabulary, Pronunciation ✣

1. **common**: happening often; frequent; ordinary
2. **a divorce**: when a marriage ends, legally
3. **legal**: lawful
4. **a marriage**: a wedding; the legal union two people
5. **a maternity leave**: a woman leaves work to have a baby and takes some time to stay home with the baby
6. **to seek**: to look for; to want

Prediction ✣ *In this dictation you are not going to listen first. Work by yourself or with a partner and fill in each blank with a word you think is correct. When you are finished, listen and do the dictation on the next page. Then compare your answers. Remember to add the T for true and F for false next to each statement. Guess if you don't know. Work with a partner or alone. Discuss your answers with the class.*

___ 1. The most common age for ____________ to marry is 27, and for women is 26.

___ 2. 51% of ______________ are now living without a husband or partner.

___ 3. More men seek divorce __________ women.

___ 4. Parents today spend more time with their _______________ than 50 years ago.

___ 5. Most men still do not _______________ their working wives with housework.

___ 6. Same sex marriages are legal in most of the 50 ______________.

___ 7. 40% ________ marriages end in divorce.

___ 8. Older people ________ now using Internet dating more than 10 years ago.

___ 9. About one-third (1/3) of births happen outside ______ marriage.

___ 10. France, Italy, and Japan have better and longer paid maternity leaves for ______________ than the U.S.

Dictation ✤ *Listen and fill in the blanks with the words you hear. Then, with a partner, compare your prediction to the listening.*

___ 1. The most common age for ____________ to marry is 27, and for women is 26.

___ 2. 51% of ______________ are now living without a husband or partner.

___ 3. More men seek divorce __________ women.

___ 4. Parents today spend more time with their _______________ than 50 years ago.

___ 5. Most men still do not _______________ their working wives with housework.

___ 6. Same-sex marriages are legal in most of the 50 ______________.

___ 7. 40% ________ marriages end in divorce.

___ 8. Older people ________ now using Internet dating more than 10 years ago.

___ 9. About one-third (1/3) of births happen outside ______ marriage.

___ 10. France, Italy, and Japan have better and longer paid maternity leaves for ______________ than the U.S.

Discussion ✤ *With a partner, discuss the following questions. Share your answers with your class.*

1. When your teacher has given you the answers to the above statements, talk about the facts that surprised you the most.
2. In the 1950s, most women married before age 22. Can you explain why the most common age is 26 now?
3. If the fastest growing group of users of Internet dating services is people who are at least 50 years old, who are these people?
4. Compare the information in the statements above to the information you have about people in your country.

Follow-up activity ✤

Write a paragraph about this family.
Who are they?
Where do they live?
How old are they?
Do the parents work?

Lucky Numbers

full text on page 126 (cd track 37)

Introduction ✣

For the Chinese, eight is the luckiest number of all. The pronunciation of the number eight sounds like the Chinese word for good fortune.

Vocabulary, Pronunciation ✣

1. **a century**: a hundred years
2. **even numbers**: numbers like 2, 4, 6, 8, and 10
3. **fortune**: luck
4. **infinite**: never-ending
5. **Judaism**: the religion of Jewish people
6. **odd numbers**: Numbers like 1, 3, 5, 7, and 9
7. **prosperity**: wealth, riches

Prediction ✣

In this dictation you are not going to listen first. Work with a partner and fill in each blank with a word you think is correct. When you are finished, listen and do the dictation on the next page. Then compare your answers.

The opening day _______ the Beijing Olympics ____________ August 8, 2008, or 08/08/08. Many couples planned _________ marry on that __________________. In Beijing 17,000 couples got married. In the United States, Las Vegas hotels advertised $888 wedding packages.

The _______________ seven in many parts of the __________________ is also a very ____________ number. Many ________________ thought the luckiest ____________ of the century was July 7, 2007 (07/07 ______), and more people married _______ that Saturday than on any _______ before that time.

Eighteen (18) ________ a lucky number in Judaism because the letters of the word "chai," which means "life," add up _________ 18. When people give money as a gift, they might _________ 18 dollars or 36 ________________ or even 180 ________________.

Dictation ✤ *Listen and fill in the blanks with the words you hear. Then, with a partner, compare your prediction to the listening.*

The opening day _______ the Beijing Olympics ___________ August 8, 2008, or 08/08/08. Many couples planned _________ marry on that _________________. In Beijing 17,000 couples got married. In the United States, Las Vegas hotels advertised $888 wedding packages.

The ______________ seven in many parts of the _________________ is also a very ____________ number. Many _______________ thought the luckiest ____________ of the century was July 7, 2007 (07/07 ______), and more people married _______ that Saturday than on any ______ before that time.

Eighteen (18) ________ a lucky number in Judaism because the letters of the word "chai," which means "life," add up _________ 18. When people give money as a gift, they might _________ 18 dollars or 36 _______________, or even 180 ________________.

Discussion ✤ *With a partner, discuss the following questions.*

1. Do you believe in lucky and unlucky numbers?
2. What are some lucky and unlucky numbers in your country?
3. Have you ever planned a special event (a party, a wedding, etc.) around a lucky number?

Follow-up activity ✤ *Some of these statements are true. Some are false. With a partner, decide which are true and which are false. The teacher will tell you the answers at the end of the activity.*

1. ___ Many hotel floors go up to 12 and then the next floor is 14.
2. ___ September 9 is the day for the "Old People's festival" in China because "9" sounds like the word for "short time" in Chinese.
3. ___ Even numbers are generally luckier than odd numbers in many cultures.
4. ___ The Chinese don't like the number "4" because it sounds like the word for "death."
5. ___ Most gamblers believe in lucky and unlucky numbers.
6. ___ All cultures have the same lucky numbers.
7. ___ It can cost a lot of money to get a lucky number for a telephone number or a license plate for a car.
8. ___ It is unlucky to have 11 people around a dinner table.
9. ___ An Asian would like to live at 444 Main Street.
10. ___ In Islamic tradition, "7" means "infinity."

Famous Immigrants in the U.S.

full text on page 127 (cd track 38)

Introduction ✣

There are many immigrants who have come to the United States and become famous. Some of them are actors, singers, scientists, musicians, athletes, writers, and architects. Do you know these names? Who are they and where did they emigrate from?

I. M. Pei	Maria Von Trapp	Martina Navratilova
Albert Einstein	Iman	Andy Garcia

Vocabulary, Pronunciation ✣

1. **an architect**: a person who designs buildings
2. **knowledge**: the learning you have or will get; information
3. **a widower**: a man whose wife has died

Prediction ✣ *Here are two short biographies of I. M.Pei and Maria Von Trapp. In this dictation you are not going to listen first. Work with a partner and fill in each blank with a word you think is correct. When you are finished you will listen and do the dictation on the next page. Then compare your answers.*

1. **I. M. Pei** is ____ famous and successful architect. He _____ born in Guangzhou, China, ____ 1917 and came to the U.S. when _____ was 17. He _____________ architecture at M.I.T. _______ worked _____ an assistant professor _____ Harvard. Some _____ the buildings Pei has designed ______ the John F. Kennedy Library ____ Boston, the Museum of Islamic Arts _____ Doha, Qatar, and ______ Bank of China Tower ____ Hong Kong.

2. **Maria Von Trapp** is famous for ______ book, *The Story of the Trapp Family,* which later ___________ the Broadway musical and popular movie, *The Sound of Music.* _______ married the widower Baron Von Trapp, ______ had seven children. With _______ musical knowledge she formed a family singing group and _________ on concert tours _______ Europe. Maria ________ from Vienna, Austria, but she and her ___________ left Austria after the Nazis took over the country in 1939.

I. M. Pei's Museum of Islamic Art in Doha, Qatar

Dictation ✤ *Check to hear if the words you have written are the same or similar to the ones you heard. Correct and discuss your dictation with a partner.*

1. **I. M. Pei** is ____ famous and successful architect. He _____ born in Guangzhou, China, ____ 1917 and came to the U.S. when _____ was 17. He _____________ architecture at M.I.T. _______ worked _____ an assistant professor _____ Harvard. Some _____ the buildings Pei has designed ______ the John F. Kennedy Library ____ Boston, the Museum of Islamic Arts _____ Doha, Qatar, and ______Bank of China Tower ____ Hong Kong.

2. **Maria Von Trapp** is famous for ______ book, *The Story of the Trapp Family,* which later ___________ the Broadway musical and popular movie, *The Sound of Music.* _______ married the widower Baron Von Trapp, ______ had seven children. With _______ musical knowledge she formed a family singing group and _________ on concert tours _______ Europe. Maria ________ from Vienna, Austria, but she and her ___________ left Austria after the Nazis took over the country in 1939.

Discussion ✤ *With a partner, discuss the following questions.*

1. Do you know of any other buildings that I. M. Pei has designed in ________?
   a. Montreal, Canada b. Dallas, Texas c. Singapore d. Taiwan

2. Name some reasons why immigrants come to the U.S.

3. Match these famous immigrants with the country they came from. You get extra points if you can say why these people are famous.

___ 1. Levi Strauss	a. The Dominican Republic
___ 2. Arnold Schwarzenegger	b. Ireland
___ 3. Gloria Estefan	c. Austria
___ 4. Bono	d. Germany
___ 5. Pedro Martinez	e. Cuba

Follow-up activity ✤ *Write a short biography of one of the famous immigrants mentioned in this unit. Use the internet to help you. Then tell the class what you have learned.*

International Baseball

full text on page 128 (cd track 39

Introduction ✤

Are you a baseball player? A baseball fan? Is baseball a popular sport in your country? Do you like the game?

Vocabulary, Pronunciation ✤

1. **a century**: one hundred years
2. **gracious**: polite and generous
3. **passionate**: having very strong feelings
4. **priceless**: very valuable
5. **professional**: doing a job, sport or activity for money

Prediction ✤ *In this dictation you are not going to listen first. Work with a partner and fill in each blank with a word you think is correct. When you are finished, listen and do the dictation on the next page. Then compare your answers.*

The national ______________ of the United ______________ __________ baseball, but ___________________ is played in many ___________________ around the globe, over 100, in fact.

For many ______________ until 2008, baseball was an international __________________ at the summer Olympics.

For example, _______ the year 2000 Team USA ______________ Cuba at the Olympic Games in Sydney, ___________________. In 2008 Korea___________ the Gold Medal at the Olympic Games in Beijing, _________________.

Because baseball is played around the ______________, on any American professional team such as the ___________________ Red Sox or the ___________ ___________ Yankees, many players are from _____________________ like Cuba, the Dominican Republic, Venezuela, Canada, Korea, and Japan as well as _____________ others.

If you are interested in playing ____________________, traveling around the world, meeting new _________________, and combining ____________________ with vacations, you should contact International.Baseball.info and you may be able to do all of those things.

Dictation ✤ *Listen and fill in the blanks with the words you hear. Then, with a partner, compare your prediction to the listening.*

The national ______________ of the United ______________ _________ baseball, but __________________ is played in many __________________ around the globe, over 100, in fact.

For many _____________ until 2008, baseball was an international _________________ at the summer Olympics.

For example, _______ the year 2000 Team USA ______________ Cuba at the Olympic Games in Sydney, _________________. In 2008 Korea___________ the Gold Medal at the Olympic Games in Beijing, ________________.

Because baseball is played around the _____________, on any American professional team such as the __________________ Red Sox or the ___________ ___________ Yankees, many players are from ____________________ like Cuba, the Dominican Republic, Venezuela, Canada, Korea, and Japan as well as _____________ others.

If you are interested in playing ____________________, traveling around the world, meeting new ________________, and combining ____________________ with vacations you should contact International.Baseball.info and you may be able to do all of those things.

Listening ✤ *Listen to the conversation between Peter and David. Then write "T" for "True" and "F" for "False" next to the following statements.*

____ 1. This year David went to Italy to play baseball and travel.
____ 2. Last year he went to Cuba.
____ 3. Some of the places he went to in Cuba were Rome and Florence.
____ 4. David plays professional baseball.
____ 5. David says he got to see a different culture in Cuba.
____ 6. David took his wife and his son with him to Italy.
____ 7. The trip was probably expensive.

Discussion ✤ *With a partner, discuss the following questions.*

1. Do you play or have you ever played baseball? Do you like to watch baseball?
2. Is baseball played in your country?
3. Which of the following sports do you prefer to watch: baseball, basketball, football, hockey, or soccer? Why?
4. If you had a son, would you prefer that he played football or baseball? Why?

Follow-up activity ✤ *Choose one.*

1. *Go to the sites* InternationalBaseball.net *and* InternationalBaseball.info. *Find out all you can about baseball adventures, and present the information to the class.*
2. *Write about a time you were on a sports team.*
3. *Find the name of the pro baseball team in your city or state. Then find the names of the players who were not born in the United States. Where are they from? Present this information to the class.*

Partial Dictations

Script for The Olympic Games Dictation on page 1 (cd track 1)

1. The very first Olympic Games **started in** Greece almost 3,000 years ago. In those early years there were simple foot races **and** horse races. **The games** honored the god Zeus and **other gods** in the town of Olympia. These games **continued** for 600 **years** and then **stopped** because people stopped believing in **many gods**.

2. The modern games **began** again in 1896 in Athens, Greece, with 250 athletes from **14** countries. Women entered the Olympics **a year later**. In the 2004 Summer Olympics in Athens, there were 11,000 athletes from 202 **different countries**.

3. The Olympic flag has **five rings**. The colors on the rings are **red, white**, blue, green, yellow, and black **because** each country in the Olympics has at least one of these colors in its national **flag**. What colors **are in** your country's flag?

Script for About Lying

Dictation on page 3 (cd track 2)

Dictation, Part 1

___ 1. Some people lie because **they are** ashamed to tell the truth.
___ 2. **Sometimes** we lie to protect other people.
___ 3. Politicians lie **a lot.**
___ 4. **Men** lie more than **women**.

Dictation, Part 2

Decide if the following lies are serious (S) or not-so-serious (NSS). Explain why.

___ 1. You **didn't do** your homework because you went **to a party** the night before. To your teacher you say, "**I was sick**."

___ 2. Bob and his **girlfriend**, Mary, are going to get married **next year,** but he went out with another girl last Saturday. When Mary **asked him** where he was on Saturday, Bob said, "I was **at the library**."

___ 3. Your **sister** just had a baby boy. When you first see the baby, **you think** he's ugly, but you look at your sister and say, "**He's** cute!"

___ 4. Susan wrote on her resumé that she graduated **from** Harvard University. She took **one course** there.

Here are some comments by Rita Kai from a Forbes *article online:*

Most of us want to be "nice," but we lie most often for selfish reasons even if at first glance it might look like "being nice." We want to be liked. That's not altruistic. We want to avoid unpleasant confrontations. That's not altruistic. We want to get on a good side of people, so they'll do favors for us. That's not altruistic either.

Script for Five Things That Will Disappear *Dictation on page 5 (cd track 3)*

Dictation

1. **The Post Office**

   Can you imagine a world **without the post office**? They are in serious financial trouble **because of e-mail**, Federal Express (FedEx), and United Parcel Service (UPS), which delivers packages. Every day most of our mail is **junk mail and bills**.

2. **The Check**

   It costs the financial system **billions of dollars** a year to process checks. This connects directly to the death **of the post office**. If you never **paid your bills by mail** and never received them by mail, the post office would definitely **go out of business**.

3. **The Land Line Telephone**

   All the cell phone companies will let you make calls using the same cell provider **for no charge** against your minutes. If you have a large family and **make a lot of local calls**, you may need a land line, but **you are paying twice** for that extra service.

4. **The Newspaper**

   People under 40 don't **read the newspaper**; they get their news online. Many don't subscribe to a daily delivered print edition. **The number of people reading** the paper online is due to the rise in Internet devices, and companies **like Apple and Amazon** have developed a model for paid subscription services.

5. **Privacy**

   Privacy **has been gone** for a long time. There are cameras on the street, **in most buildings**, and even built into your computer **or cell phone**. You can be sure that 24/7, "they" know who you are **and where you are**.

Script for Wild Turkeys

Dictation on page 8 (cd track 4)

Dictation

People began to see wild turkeys in cities **a few years ago**. They were very excited and took lots of photos. Now that there are so many of these large birds, people are not so happy. Some people are afraid **of them**. Here is a story about Mrs. Rosen.

One day Mrs. Rosen, **a teacher**, got off the bus **to go to** the bank in her city. She felt something poke **her in the back**. She turned around and saw a big wild turkey. She began to run, and the turkey **ran after her**. At the bank she turned around and screamed very loudly at the turkey, "**Go away**!" The turkey turned around and slowly started to cross the street. All traffic stopped. Cars honked **their horns**. The turkey didn't care. It wasn't **in a hurry**. It walked very slowly until it got to the sidewalk.

One wildlife official said that if you run from turkeys as Mrs. Rosen did, **they will follow you** because they think it's a game.

Script for Tipping in a Restaurant

Dictation on page 10 (cd track 5)

Dictation

Check	15%	20%
$20.00	3.00	4.00
$35.00	5.25	**7.00**
$58.00	**8.70**	11.60
$72.00	10.80	**14.40**
$86.00	**12.90**	17.20
$97.00	14.55	**19.40**

Note to teachers:

Some students, when going to restaurants, resist tipping because it is not a custom in their country. They do not understand or accept the reasoning behind it.

In the follow-up activities, the students are asked to find out what tip is appropriate for a hairdresser, a taxi driver, a hotel bellhop, a pizza delivery person, a manicurist, or a newspaper delivery person. They will come up with a variety of answers from asking people or researching on the Internet. A 10% to 15% tip is reasonable, but students will come up with other opinions which they can discuss.

Script for Changing Careers

Dictation on page 12 (cd track 6)

Terry and Kanji in their store

Dictation

In **2001** a friend gave Terry a **little dog** as a gift. She named him Kanji. Terry's life changed. She had **to come home** earlier to take care of Kanji. He made her feel better. She was healthier and happier.

In **2004** she decided it was time for a change. She quit her **job** and decided to open a store that sold things for dogs and cats. She had saved **a lot of money** so she didn't have to borrow any. For a year she went to classes on how to start a small business. Then she found a **small** empty store near **her house.**

She **sells** many useful things and many things that are not as useful. One of her best-selling items **for dogs** is rubber boots that look like balloons. They are important in the winter so that dogs don't get sand and salt in their paws when they **walk** on icy streets. She also **sells** things like **baseball** jackets **for dogs** and T-shirts that say, "Dogs are children in fur coats." She says that she **has never been** happier.

Chronological Order

8 5 3 1 6 2 4 7

Dog Idioms

1. It's very hot.
2. He's too old to learn something new.
3. He's very sick.
4.. It's raining very hard.
5, Don't change things, or they may get worse.
6. I'll take the left-over food home from the restaurant.
7. This situation is very difficult.

Script for Greeting Cards

Dictation on page 14 (cd track 7)

Dictation

Hallmark **is the largest** greeting card company **in the United States**. The company started **in 1910**. It makes about **19,000 new cards** a year. About **16,000** people **work** for the company. The average person sends about **55 cards** a year.

Now **you can buy** musical cards that **play songs** like "Happy Birthday to You" when you open them. You can **also send** electronic greeting cards (e-cards) or send greetings to a mobile **phone** by text message.

In August **2008** Hallmark began **to make** same-sex marriage cards for states where same-sex marriage is legal.

The company's motto is "When you care enough to send **the very best**."

Listening

M: Can I ask you a few questions?

S: Sure. Why not?

M: My first question is: how often do you buy and send greeting cards?

S: That's a good question. I have to think about it. I send about twenty cards a year, and maybe another twenty cards at Christmas.

M: How much do you usually spend on a card?

S: Usually about $2.95. At Christmas time I buy a box of cards. Then they're much cheaper.

M: What was the last card you sent?

S: Unfortunately last week I had to send a sympathy card to a friend. Her father had died. I also sent a get-well card to someone in my office who has a broken leg.

M: Did you send her a serious card or a funny card?

S: I sent her a funny card.

M: When did you last get a card?

S: On my birthday. I got cards from my husband, all of my children, from friends, and one from everyone in the office. Almost all of the cards made fun of me getting older.

M: Those cards are very popular now. We even have cards for people who are becoming 90 or 100.

S: That's amazing!

M: It is. Thank you for your time. You've been very helpful.

True or False

1: F 2: T 3: F 4: T 5: F

Script for Trivia Contests *Dictation on page 16 (cd track 8)*

Dictation

1. Where can **you buy** a Whopper Junior?
2. Who **wrote** *Romeo and Juliet*?
3. What language do **people in** Mexico speak?
4. How much does a pack of cigarettes **cost**?
5. Where is the longest **river** in the world located?
6. How long **does** it **take** to fly from New York to London?
7. How much is **ten bucks**?
8. What does "I **get it**" mean?
9. Where are the next Summer Olympics **going to be**?
10. **You are** invited to a potluck party. What does potluck mean?

Answers to the trivia questions:

1. Burger King
2. Shakespeare
3. Spanish
4. (check locally)
5. Africa (Nile)
6. about seven hours
7. ten dollars
8. "I undersand."
9. Rio in 2016, Tokyo in 2020
10. Everyone brings something to eat.

Follow-up answers to "Fact and Opinion":

1. fact 2. opinion 3. opinion 4. fact 5. fact

6. opinion 7. fact 8. opinion 9. fact 10. opinion

Note to teachers:

This activity works even better if teachers create their own trivia items tailor made for their class.

Follow-up answers to "Top Five":

1. The five largest countries in area: Russia, Canada, China, U.S., Brazil
2. The five countries in population: China, India, U.S., Indonesia, Brazil
3. The five countries with the longest life expectancies: Andorra, San Marino, Japan, Singapore, Australia
4. The five car-producing countries: Japan, Germany, U.S., France, South Korea
5. The five countries with the most people per household: Iraq, Equatorial Guinea, Pakistan, Yemen, Solomon Islands.

Script for Languages in the U.S.

Dictation on page 18 (cd track 9)

Dictation

The population of the United States **is** 325,000,000. Most people speak English, but the Census Bureau tells us that **there are** 14 million U.S. households where people speak **a language** other than English. In the state of California, more than **one** language is spoken in 40% of the households **there**. Nationwide, one in five children enters **school** speaking a language other than English.

Unfortunately, these **students** often lose much of their first language when they **learn English**. When immigrant students are in high school and have been in the U.S. since they were **four** or **five**, many of them can still **understand** their first language, but they cannot read **or write** in their first language.

Follow-up activity answers:

1a. Spanish is spoken in: Mexico, Guatemala, Honduras, Costa Rica, Panama, Puerto Rico, Cuba, Nicaragua, Venezuela, Colombia, Peru, Paraguay, Uruguay, Argentina, Chile, Ecuador, Spain, Bolivia, El Salvador, the Dominican Republic, and the U.S.

1b. English is spoken in the U.S., Canada, Australia, England, Scotland, Ireland, Wales, New Zealand, Bermuda, South Africa, Belize, and Fiji. It is also widely spoken as an official language in many other countries such as Botswana, Namibia, Ghana, and the Commonwealth of Caribbean Nations.

1c. Arabic is spoken in Algeria, Bahrain, Chad, Djibouti, Egypt, Ethiopia, Iraq, Jordan, Kuwait, Lebanon, Libya, Mauritania, Morocco, Oman, Qatar, Saudi Arabia, Somalia, Syria, Tunisia, United Arab Emirates, and Yemen.

Script for Valentine's Day Around the World

Dictation on page 20 (cd track 10)

Dictation

1. **The Dominican Republic and El Salvador**

   In these countries, friends and family **play games**. In the Dominican Republic, **the game** is called *Angelito,* and in El Salvador it is called *Amigo Secreto* (secret friend). Friends write **the name** of another person (boy or girl) on a small piece of paper. Then each player **gives** this friend a **gift**.

2. **Italy and Britain**

   Young women stand by **the window** in the early morning on Valentine's Day. They believe that **the first man** they see will be their husband!

3. **Japan**

   Japan **has two** Valentine's Days. On February 14th, **girls give** dark chocolate to the boys **they like**, and on March 14th, **boys give** cookies or **white** chocolate to the girls they like.

Dictogloss and Partial Dictations

Script for The Youngest College Professor *Dictation on page 22 (cd track 11)*

Dictogloss

1. She could read and talk at eight months old.
2. She finished high school at age eight.
3. She graduated from the university when she was 14.

Dictation

When Alia graduated from Stony Brook University in New York, **she was** the youngest woman in U.S. history to do so. Her education continued at Drexel University **in** Pennsylvania, where **she received** her Master's and a Ph.D. in materials science and engineering. She **chose teaching** because she feels she can help **a lot of** people.

Note to teachers:

Alia Sabur's grandparents are from Iran. In 2008 Alia took a position at Konkuk University in Seoul, South Korea.

Answers to the Brain Teasers, Discussion 2:

1. She was walking.
2. There are more Chinese than Japanese.
3. Bobby
4. All of them

Script for How Green Are You? *Dictation on page 24 (cd track 12)*

Dictation

1. With your car:
   I don't **drive**. I take the bus **or train** to work.

2. With your food:
   I eat more vegetables **and fruit** than I used to.

3. With your waste:
   a. I recycle newspapers, **glass, cans**, and plastic.

4. With your purchases:
   a. I try to buy products that **are** environmentally friendly, even if they are **more expensive.**

Dictogloss

1. I plan to buy a hybrid car.
2. I eat less meat than I used to.
3. I recycle just bottles and cans.
4. I can help save the planet.

Script for Kissing

Dictation on page 26 (cd track 13)

Dictation

Anthropologists think that kissing began with **mouth**-to-**mouth** feeding of primates by their mothers. **Mothers** may have chewed **the food** first and then **put it** in their babies' mouths. Mother birds **bring their babies** food in their beaks. This is called beak-to-beak feeding. **Some people** see this as kissing.

Dictogloss

1. The first movie kiss was in 1896.
2. In writing, a kiss is written as an "X."
3. When you kiss, you use 36 muscles.
4. There are some places in the world where people do not kiss.

Follow-up: the meanings of the Kiss Idioms

2a. Let's be friends again.
2b. Someone will take your purse.
2c. He said goodbye to her by touching his lips.
2d. Chocolate kisses are candy.

Note to teachers:

There are other frequently used "kiss" expressions which students often ask about, like "kiss my ass," "kiss ass" and "kiss up to." When students ask, we explain their meanings.

Script for Soap Operas *Dictation on page 28 (cd track 14)*

Dictation

Soap operas are popular **in** countries **all over the world.** For example, people **in both Japan** and Korea enjoy watching Korean soap operas. People in **both** Turkey and Greece **enjoy** watching Turkish soap operas.

India **has many soap** operas in **many** different languages. **They** became popular in the late 1980s as more people **began to buy** televisions. At **the beginning** of the 21st century, soap operas **became** an important part of Indian culture. **Many of these** are about **love** and **arranged marriages.**

Dictogloss

1. The slang for "soap operas" is "the soaps."
2. Soap operas are very popular in many countries.
3. People are starting to watch soap operas on the Internet.

Follow-up: Punctuation

Tiffany loves Derek, but Derek only loves Tiffany like a sister. He loves Claudia. She is not a very good woman and only likes Derek because he has a lot of money. It is May. Derek and Claudia are going to have a big wedding in June. They have invited three hundred people. Will Tiffany come to the wedding?

Script for Traffic *Dictation on page 30 (cd track 16)*

Dictation

A cop pulls over a carload of women.

Cop: This is a **65** MPH highway. Why **are you going** so slowly?
Woman: Sir, I saw a lot of signs that said 22, not 65.
Cop: That's not the speed limit. **That's the name** of the highway you're on.
Woman: Oh, silly me! **Thanks** for letting me know. I'll be more careful.

At this point the cop looks in the backseat, where the other women are shaking and trembling.

Cop: Excuse me, **what's wrong with** your friends back there? They're shaking terribly.
Woman: Oh, we just got off of Highway **119**.

Dictogloss

1. Men honk more than women.
2. Most accidents happen on clear dry days.
3. Drivers honk more on weekends.

Script for Oprah's School in South Africa

Dictation on page 32 (cd track 16)

Dictation

The Oprah Winfrey Leadership Academy **is open to** poor girls who want **to learn** and become leaders. Classes at the school **are small,** with only 15 students. Teachers come from **many different** countries to share their knowledge and ideas. The school has **28 buildings**, including computer and science labs, dormitories, and a health center. Tuition **is free**.

Dictogloss

1. More than 3,000 girls applied to the school.
2. Oprah interviewed 500 girls.
3. She teaches a course via satellite.

Script for **Overworked** *Dictation on page 34 (cd track 17)*

Dictation

Karoshi is the Japanese phrase for "death from **overwork**." Thirty years ago the Japanese government **realized** that workers who work for **up to 12 hours** a day, six or seven **days a week**, year **after year**, might die from overwork. A government officer can decide if the person died from overwork. Then the family will be paid money. South Koreans, who have the **longest working hours** in the world, call death by work *kwarosa*.

Dictogloss

1. The workweek in many countries is 40 hours.
2. France has a 35-hour workweek.
3. Many people have three to five weeks of vacation every year.

Script for Stay-at-Home Dads

Dictation on page 13 (cd track 7)

Pre-listening Dictogloss

1. The number of stay-at-home dads is increasing.
2. Day care can cost $28,000 a year for two kids.
3. Many wives make more money than their husbands.

Listening script

Q. Jack, you're a stay-at-home dad. Was it an easy decision to make?

A. Actually, yes it was, because my wife and I believe that parents, not a day care center, should raise their children. And we think children are happier at home with a parent.

Q. Usually it's the mother who stays at home. Why did you decide to be the one to stay at home?

A. I lost my job with General Motors. We are lucky that my wife, as a teacher, makes a good salary (better than mine) and was happy to go back to work.

Q. So you can live on one salary?

A. Well, yes, but we have to be very careful how we spend our money.

Q. So, for now, it's OK?

A. Yes. . . I'll go back to work when the twins are in elementary school. For now, it's working out, but I'll tell you, being a full-time daddy is not easy!!!

Answer Key for Listening

T 1. It was an easy decision for Jack to stay at home.
F 2. Day care centers are too expensive for Jack and his wife.
T 3. Jack thinks children are happier at home with a parent.
T 4. His wife makes a pretty good salary.
F 5. Jack used to work as a teacher.
F 6. Living on one salary is not working out.
T 7. His wife was happy to go back to work.
T 8. Jack plans to go back to work when the twins go to school.
F 9. Being a full-time dad at home is easy.
F 10. When he goes back to work, his wife will stay home.

Script for **A Courageous Athlete**

Dictation on page 38 (cd track 19)

Dictation

In **2013** Tatyana McFadden, a talented 24-year-old disabled athlete, became **the first person to win** all four major marathons **in a year (Boston, London**, Chicago, **and New York**). In 2014 she won the Boston marathon again.

She **was born** in Russia in 1988 with spina bifida (a hole in her spine), which left her paralyzed **below the waist**. For the **first six years** of her life she had **to walk** on her hands **and her feet** because she lived in a poor orphanage and didn't have a wheelchair.

In 1994 she was adopted by Debbie McFadden, an American, and began to **do many sports** like swimming and gymnastics to strengthen her muscles. She has competed in many **sports**, has won many medals, and **has also been** active in **helping** disabled athletes **get** the right to compete.

Dictogloss

1. She started marathon racing in 2009.
2. In the 2014 Olympics, she won a silver medal for skiing.
3. She moved from Russia to the United States when she was six.

Note: You might want to do this dictation in conjunction with ***International Adoptions***.

Pair Dictations

Script for Are You a Shopaholic? *Dictation on page 40 (cd track 20)*

Dictation

1. When I feel sad, I often go shopping.
2. I spend a lot of money that I do not have on things that I do not need.
3. I have closets full of clothes that I almost never wear.
4. I feel very excited and happy when I buy something, but soon I feel tired and sad.
5. I often don't tell my family and my friends about how much I spent, or I tell them that I have spent less than I really have.

Script for Three Wishes *Dictation on page 43 (cd track 21)*

Dictation

1. You are studying English as a Second Language. Choose a third language that you don't know. In a few days you will be able to listen to, speak, read, and write this language well. What language will you choose, and why?

2. You will get a package from someone. Decide who it will be from and decide what will be in it.

3. Next month you can go anywhere in the world and take someone with you. Where will you go, and who will you take with you?

Script for International Adoptions

Dictation on page 45 (cd track 22)

Dictation

When Americans (single or married) want a family but they cannot have a child of their own, they often decide to adopt. Sometimes Americans go to other countries to find a child. They work with adoption agencies. Adoption agencies help them with information about the child, such as age, health, and gender. There are rules everyone must follow. For example, Americans must visit the country once or twice, and meet the child and the social workers. Then they can take the child home. The cost of adopting a child can be up to $30,000.

Note: You might want to do this dictation in conjunction with ***Courageous Athletes***.

Script for Names

Dictation on page 47 (cd track 23)

Dictation

There are several kinds of American names. One kind is names from jobs. Some of these popular names are Cook, Carpenter, Smith, and Baker. Another kind is names from colors. It includes names like Brown, White, and Black. We also get names that are about family, like Johnson (John's son).

Follow-up: Punctuation

In the United States the family names of many African-Americans began in slavery. Many of them were given the surnames of their owners. Many freed slaves either created family names for themselves or took the names of their former owners. Others, such as Muhammad Ali and Malcolm X, changed their names rather than live with the ones the slave owner had given to their ancestors.

Script for Overweight *Dictation on page 50 (cd track 24)*

Dictation

In 2008 the Japanese government made a law. It said that doctors and nurses would measure the waistlines of all people between the ages of 40 and 74. A man's waistline must be 33.4 inches or under. A woman's waistline must be 35.4 inches or under. If someone's waistline is too big, they must try to lose weight or take classes about nutrition and diet.

Note: *The ideal score on the "report card" would be 65.*

Listening Script

Tom: Hi, George. How are you?
George: I think I'm OK. I saw my doctor yesterday.

T: What did he say?
G: "She,"not "he." My doctor's a woman. She said I was OK but I was overweight. I've gained 10 pounds since I last saw her. She thinks I should try to lose five pounds before I see her in three months.

T: Five pounds! That's nothing!
G: She says I should exercise more and eat less and also eat less salt because my blood pressure is a little high.

T: So do it.
G: I'll try, but it's hard. I love things that are sweet or salty. So no more chocolate cookies with my lunch and no more potato chips when I'm watching TV.

T: And for exercise?
G: The doctor said I should try to exercise 30 minutes every day – so more walking and less TV and iPad.

Answers to Listening True and False Check

T 1. The doctor is a woman.
F 2. His blood pressure is a little low.
F 3. He has gained 15 pounds.
F 4. He needs to lose 10 pounds.
T 5. He needs to exercise more.
F 6. He should exercise three times a week.
T 7. He likes chocolate cookies.
F 8. He doesn't like salty foods.

Script for Coffee, Coffee, and More Coffee *Dictation on page 54 (cd track 25)*

Dictation

John "Winter" Smith, a 42-year-old computer programmer, wants to drink coffee in every Starbucks in the world. He started to do this in 1997. By 2013 he had drunk half a cup of decaffeinated coffee in 8,971 Starbucks in North America, and 2,468 Starbucks around the world. One day he visited 28 shops in one American city.

When he gets to a shop, he drinks his coffee, takes a picture of the shop, and leaves. He is not one of the people you often see at Starbucks reading books or working on their computers.

Winter selfie at Starbucks

Who is Winter?

Winter is a forty-something freelance computer software developer. This means that he can plan his work schedule so that he can travel. He has changed his name from Rafael Antonio Lozano. He drives old cars and sleeps in them to save money. In 2008 he estimated that he had spent about $30,000 in the previous 10 or so years traveling to Starbucks. He went to the University of Texas in Austin, where he got a degree in philosophy and computer science.

Script for Intermarriage *Dictation on page 57 (cd track 26)*

Dictation

One hundred years ago, most immigrants came to America from Europe. Their children went to school with non-immigrant American children. When the new Americans married, they often married Americans from other heritages.

Today, the same is true for Asian-Americans and Latinos. They often marry non-Asians and non-Latinos. For example, about one-half of Asian women marry non-Asian men. About one-third of U.S.-born Latinos marry non-Latinos.

Source:

Information taken from *The Return of the Melting Pot*, by Linda Chavez, *NY Post,* August 16, 2008.

Note to teachers:

Intermarriage is more common among second-generation immigrants.

Suggested Reading:

Stealing Buddha's Dinner, Bich Minh Nguyen. New York: Viking Penguin, 2008.
An autobiographical account of a young girl growing up in an Asian-Latino family.

Script for A Historic Day

Dictation on page 59 (cd track 27)

Introduction answers

There are different possibilities for the nine statements. Here is one:

2 8 3 1 5 4 9 7 6 10

Dictation

1. **James Carson, 64**:

   I am surprised and happy. I didn't think a black man would be President in my lifetime. When I was a child, black kids couldn't even go to the same schools as whites – before 1965.

2. **LaToya Williams, 61**:

   Martin Luther King, Jr.'s famous speech, "I have a dream," is now true for us. Obama will be President for all Americans, black and white.

3. **George Miller, 44**:

   Now I can look my son in the eye and say, "You can truly be whatever you want to be, even a U.S. President." I finally feel fully American.

Script for Medical Myths

Dictation on page 62 (cd track 28)

Dictation

Our parents and teachers told us that reading in dim light will hurt our eyes. But most eye doctors say that reading in low light does not hurt our eyes.

There are other medical myths that people believe which are not true. For example, hair and fingernails do not continue to grow after someone dies. Also, shaving hair does not make it grow back faster and darker.

Answers to the discussion questions:

a. ***True***.

b. ***False***. We can get enough fluids by drinking juice, milk, etc.

c. ***False***. Turkey does not contain enough tryptophan to make someone sleepy.

d. ***True***.

e. ***False***. Recent scientific studies show that we use much more than 10% of our brains.

f. ***True***.

g. ***False***. When our hair turns gray depends on our genes and not stress.

Script for Ken's Cadillacs *Dictation on page 64 (cd track 29)*

Dictation

"Ken's, good morning," my brother Ken said when he answered the phone at his car dealership, Ken's Cadillacs. The caller asked about their hours, and my brother explained that they opened at nine but closed between 12 and 1 p.m.

"You're saying you're closed for lunch? But that's really crazy," the woman said.

"Well, we gotta eat," Ken said.

The conversation got even more tense until they realized that the woman had the wrong number. She had been trying to reach Ken's Steakhouse!

Possible answers to the discussion questions:

If students want to name specific models, that's fine, too. Example: Honda Accord

1a. How many American cars can you name?
Cadillac, Ford, Chevrolet, Chrysler, Plymouth, Olds, etc.

1b. How many Japanese cars can you name?
Honda, Toyota, Nissan, Mitsubishi, Isuzu, Mazda, etc.

1c. How many German cars can you name?
Mercedes, Audi, Volkswagen, BMW, Smart, Porsche

Possible answers to the discussion inventing businesses to fit these names; *accept any logical answers.*

2a. ***Bob's Auto Body*** – a repair shop or garage
2b. ***The Dog House*** – a place where you can buy a hotdog; a place that sells dogs and accessories
2c. ***The Right Cut*** – a hairdresser or barber; a butcher shop
2d. ***Cool It*** – an ice cream shop; a place to buy an air conditioner
2e. ***Grandmother's Attic*** – an antique shop; a place to buy used clothes or a second-hand shop
2f. ***Sweet Pleasures*** – a candy shop; a children's toy store
2g. ***Bath and Body Works*** – a spa; a shop that sells beauty products

Script for The Top Three

Dictation on page 67 (cd track 30)

Dictation

1. What's a good food that warms you up on a cold night?
2. What is a way to get rich quick?
3. Name a way to say goodbye in another language.
4. At what age do girls start wearing lipstick?
5. Name a favorite American vacation spot.
6. What is something people do for their country?
7. Name an occupation that is always in demand.
8. Name a holiday that can be dangerous.

Dictation answers

1, a. hot chocolate b. oatmeal c. soup
2. a. inherit it c. marry money d. win the lottery
3. b. adios c. sayonara d. au revoir
4. a. 12 b. 13 c. 14
5. a. Florida b. Las Vegas d. Disneyland (or Disney World)
6. a. pay taxes b. vote c. serve in the military
7. a. soldier b. nurse c. doctor
8. a. New Year's Eve b. Memorial Day c. July 4th

Discussion answers

1. Name an animal that is black and white. (zebra, panda, skunk, dalmatian dog)
2. Name a dangerous job. (fisherman, pilot, lumberjack, policeman)
3. Name a part of the body mentioned in love songs. (heart, arms, eyes)
4. What is something people add sugar to/ (coffee, cereal, tea)
5. What do bees do? (sting, buzz, make honey)
6. Name a fruit that is the size of a tennis ball. (orange, apple, pear)
7. Name the heaviest thing in your apartment/house. (refrigerator, bed)
8. Name an age that's good to marry. (26, 27, 30)
9. What is a color you wouldn't paint your house? (pink, purple, black)
10. Name something a woman might have in her medicine cabinet. (deodorant, toothpaste, pills)
11. Name an animal that could swallow you. (whale, crocodile)
12. Name someone or something that starts with the word "lady."
    (Lady Godiva, Lady GaGa, Lady Diana, *Lady Killers* (a movie), lady bug)

Fact or Opinion

1. F 2. O 3. F 4. O 5. F 6. F 7. O

Script for **School Uniforms** *Dictation on page 70 (cd track 31)*

Dictation

When you went to school, did you ever wear a uniform? If you didn't wear one, were there any rules about what you could wear and what you couldn't wear? In most public schools in the United States there are no uniforms. However, in some towns and cities there are some things you can't wear to school. Some examples of these are flip-flops, hoodies, and baggy pants pulled down low.

Students often disagree with these rules. They say, "People should dress the way they want to dress. The way I dress is the way I express myself."

Listening

Sheila: What are you wearing to school tomorrow?

Billy: I don't know. Probably a tee shirt, jeans, and my denim jacket.

Sheila: Sometimes I think I'd like to go to a private school like my sister and brother do. They wear uniforms and don't have to worry about what they wear every day.

Billy: I'm sure I'd hate that. What does your sister wear?

Sheila: She wears a plaid skirt, a white blouse, and a green blazer. She has to wear knee socks unless it's cold. Then she wears tights.

Billy: It sounds uncomfortable. Also, would you like to look like everyone else? What about your brother?

Sheila: He wears gray trousers – no jeans, of course –, a white shirt and a tie, and a blue blazer. Also, he can't wear his baseball cap.

Billy: A tie? Does he really have to wear a tie every day?

Sheila: Yep. He hates it. As soon as he leaves school every day, he pulls off the tie and takes his baseball cap out of his backpack.

Billy: I like clothes that express the way I feel.

Sheila: Me too. I'll wear my miniskirt and a tee shirt tomorrow.

Answers to Listening

baseball cap, jeans, knee socks, skirts, tee shirts, ties, tights, white shirts

Prediction Dictations

Script for Rosa Parks

Dictation on page 73 (cd track 32)

Note to teachers:

Accept any logical or grammatical response.

Dictation

Every day for years, Rosa Parks got on **the** bus to go to work in Montgomery, Alabama. **She** always sat in the first row of the black section at the back of the **bus**. Whites sat **in** the front section. One morning as Rosa was going **to** work, the bus filled up with both whites **and** blacks. The bus driver shouted to the Negroes to give up **their** seats to the whites. Rosa did not move. She stayed in her **seat** and looked out the window. She was tired of **whites** telling her what to do. The bus driver **became** angry and called the police. The police came and took **Rosa** to jail. When the black community **heard** that Rosa was in jail, they decided to take action. With the help **of** Dr. Martin Luther King, Jr., the blacks in the **city** organized a bus boycott. 95% of the blacks in the city stopped **taking** the buses to and from work. The boycott lasted 381 days. Finally, **the** Supreme Court declared segregation on buses unconstitutional. Rosa had started **an** important revolution.

Answers to discussion of the quotations and who said them

a. the bus driver
b. Dr. Martin Luther King, Jr.
c. Rosa
d. Rosa
e. the Supreme Court

Note to teachers:

Rosa Parks was born on February 4, 1913, in Tuskegee, Alabama. In 1955 she was active in the Civil Rights Movement, but on December 1, 1955, she took her action as a private citizen "tired of giving in." Nevertheless, her simple act became a powerful political symbol, and she was given national honors later in life. She died on October 24, 2005, in Detroit, Michigan, at the age of 92. To honor her, Rosa's body was laid in state under the Rotunda of the U.S. Capitol.

Script for Asking for Advice

Dictation on page 76 (cd track 33)

Note to teachers:

Accept any logical or grammatical response.

Dictation

Dear Sandy,

I have **a** problem. I want **to** be a rock musician when I finish high school, but **my** father **says**, "No!" I play the guitar **with** a group of friends after school, and we are **going** to play for a big party **in** our town next week. I can sing pretty **well**, too. My father says, "Go to college and **study** business so you **can** help us with our family's furniture business." Sometimes I **work** in the store on weekends, but it's boring. I don't **want to** go to college. My father is not a college graduate, so **this** is important to him. All I want to do is **play** the guitar and sing with my **friends**. What can I do?

Johnny Jagger

Script for Fact or Opinion

Dictation on page 78 (cd track 34)

Dictation

F 1. The Pacific Ocean is **the** largest of the four oceans.

F 2. The oldest university in the world **is** in Morocco.

O 3. Chinese **is** more difficult to learn than Arabic.

O 4. Paris is the most beautiful **city** in Europe.

F 5. A Honda Civic is less expensive **than** a Honda Accord.

O 6. Democracy is the best form **of** government.

F 7. Haiti is the poorest **country** in the Western Hemisphere.

O 8. History is more **interesting** than science.

O 9. Cancer is the worst **disease** that a person can have.

F 10. John F. Kennedy **was** the youngest man ever elected President **of the** United States.

Note to teachers:

Theodore Roosevelt was younger than Kennedy when he took office, but he was elected Vice-President and became President when William McKinley was assassinated in 1901.

Script for Giant Pandas

Dictation on page 80 (cd track 35)

Dictation

Visitors to zoos think that giant **pandas are** very cute, especially baby **pandas**. Pandas **have** fur which is black and white. They are about three **feet** tall (91 centimeters) when they are standing on their four **legs**.

Males weigh up to 250 **pounds** (110 kilograms). Females usually weigh less than 220 **pounds** (100 **kilograms**).

Pandas **eat** as much as 40 pounds (18 **kilograms**) of bamboo every **day**. They spend ten to sixteen **hours** every **day** looking for **food** and eating it. In zoos **giant** pandas eat some vegetables and fruit as well as **bamboo**.

The female **panda** is ready to mate only once a **year** for **two** or three days in the spring. She will have one or **two** cubs. Often only **one** will survive.

Script for American Families

Dictation on page 82 (cd track 336)

Dictation

true 1. The most common age for **men** to marry is 27, and for women is 26.

true 2. 51% of **women** are now living without a husband or partner.

false 3. More men seek divorce **than** women.

true 4. Parents today spend more time with their **children** than 50 years ago.

false 5. Most men still do not **help** their working wives with housework.

false 6. Same-sex marriages are legal in most of the 50 **states**.

true 7. 40% **of** marriages end in divorce.

true 8. Older people **are** now using Internet dating more than 10 years ago.

true 9. About one-third (1/3) of births happen outside **of** marriage.

true 10. France, Italy, and Japan have better and longer paid maternity leaves for **women** than the U.S.

Script for Lucky Numbers

Dictation on page 84 (cd track 37)

Dictation

The opening day **of** the Beijing Olympics **was** August 8, 2008, or 08/08/08. Many couples planned **to** marry on that **day**. In Beijing 17,000 couples got married. In the United States, Las Vegas hotels advertised $888 wedding packages.

The **number** seven in many parts of the **world** is also a very **lucky** number. Many **people** thought the luckiest **day** of the century was July 7, 2007 (07/07/**07**), and more people married **on** that Saturday than on any **day** before that time.

Eighteen **is** a lucky number in Judaism because the letters of the word *chai,* which means "life," add up **to** 18. When people give money as a gift, they might **give** 18 dollars or 36 **dollars,** or even 180 **dollars.**

Prediction activity

1. ***True.*** This is because "13" is the unluckiest number in Western culture.
2. ***False.*** The word for "nine" means "Long time."
3. ***True.***
4. ***True.***
5. ***True.***
6. ***False.***
7. ***True.***
8. ***False.*** It is unlucky to have 13 people around a dinner table.
9. ***False.*** For most Asians, "4" is the worst number.
10. ***True.***

Script for Famous Immigrants in the U.S. *Dictation on page 86 (cd track 38)*

Introduction answers

Iman, a supermodel, is from Somalia.
Andy Garcia is an actor from Cuba.
Martina Navratilova is a famous tennis player from The Czech Republic.

Dictation

1. **I. M. Pei** is **a** famous and successful architect. He **was** born in Guangzhou, China, **in** 1917 and came to the U.S. when **he** was 17. He **studied** architecture at M.I.T. **and** worked **as** an assistant professor **at** Harvard. Some **of** the buildings Pei has designed **are** the John F. Kennedy Library **in** Boston, the Museum of Islamic Arts **in** Doha, Qatar, and **the** Bank of China Tower **in** Hong Kong.

2. **Maria Von Trapp** is famous for **her** book, *The Story of the Trapp Family,* which later **became** the Broadway musical and popular movie, *The Sound of Music.* **She** married the widower Baron Von Trapp, **who** had seven children. With **her** musical knowledge she formed a family singing group and **went** on concert tours **in** Europe. Maria **came** from Vienna, Austria, but she and her **family** left Austria after the Nazis took over the country in 1939.

Note to teachers:

The Trapp family moved to Vermont in the United States. Maria died in 1987 at the age of 82.

Answers to the discussion quiz

Levi Strauss – Germany
Arnold Schwarzenegger – Austria
Gloria Estefan – Cuba
Bono – Ireland
Pedro Martinez – The Dominican Republic

Script for **International Baseball** *Dictation on page 89 (cd track 39)*

Dictation

The national **sport** of the United **States is** baseball, but **baseball** is played in many **countries** around the globe, over 100, in fact.

For many **years**, until 2008, baseball was an international sport at the Summer Olympics. For example, **in** the year 2000 Team USA **beat** Cuba at the Olympic Games in Sydney, **Australia**. In 2008 Korea **won** the Gold Medal at the Olympic Games in Beijing, **China**.

Because baseball is played around the **world**, on any American professional team such as the **Boston** Red Sox or the **New York** Yankees, many players are from **countries** like Cuba, the Dominican Republic, Venezuela, Canada, Korea, and Japan as well as **many** others.

If you are interested in playing **baseball**, traveling around the world, meeting new **friends**, and combining **baseball** with vacations, you should contact InternationalBaseball.info and you may be able to do all of those things.

Listening

Peter: Hi. How's it going?

David: Okay, I guess. It's hard being back at work. I'm tired. But I had a fantastic vacation.

Peter: Where'd you go?

David: The three of us – my wife, my daughter Mary, and I – went to Italy for two weeks with a baseball adventure group. I played baseball with a bunch of great guys, and the team and the families toured Milan, Verona, Florence, and Rome. The people, the friends, the food – all of it was priceless, and my wife and daughter had a great time.

Peter: Didn't you do something like this last year?

David: Two years ago. We went to Cuba. They love baseball there. We played against some of the most passionate players in the world. Every day was an adventure. We saw a different culture, and every person we met was warm and gracious.

Peter: How do you arrange this trip? Will you go next year?

David: We travel with a baseball adventure group that makes all the arrangements. They say, "Play baseball. See the world." Unfortunately I can only afford to go every second year or every third year,.

Cuba-Canada 2009

Answers to Listening True and False Check

T 1. This year David went to Italy to play baseball and travel.

F 2. Last year he went to Cuba.

F 3. Some of the places he went to in Cuba were Rome and Florence.

F 4. David plays professional baseball.

T 5. David says he got to see a different culture in Cuba.

F 6. David took his wife and his son with him to Italy.

T 7. The trip was probably expensive.

Other Books from Pro Lingua

Three other books of dictations by Catherine Sadow and Judy DeFilippo

Basic Dictations (launched beginner), **Interactive Dictations** (intermediate), and **Dictations for Discussion** (high-intermediate to advanced). In the first book, the subject of the dictations is basic information about U.S. culture that will help newcomers succeed. In the more advanced books, as in **Great Dictations**, the students are given a newspaper or magazine article in dictation; several dictation techniques are used, all involving filling in blanks in a gapped text. After checking their work with each other, they discuss the articles, and then there are varied writing and follow-up assignments. Listening to the articles read by native speakers on CD helps build listening comprehension.

Conversation Strategies. 29 structured pair activities for developing strategic conversation skills at the intermediate level. Students learn the words, phrases, and conventions used by native speakers in the active give-and-take of everyday conversation.

Discussion Strategies. Carefully structured pair and small-group work at the advanced-intermediate level. Excellent preparation for students who will participate in academic or professional work that requires effective participation in discussions and seminars.

In My Opinion. 50 contemporary, thought-provoking topics presented in two basic photocopyable formats. Just over half of them are in the form of a questionnaire that students fill out and/or respond to orally. Then they compare responses and discuss the "gaps" between their views – what is good/bad, right/wrong, liberal/conservative, and so on. The other activities use opinion cards, 12 to a page, asking the cardholder to voice an opinion to be agreed with or challenged by the others in the class.

Conversation Inspirations. A photocopyable collection of over 2400 conversation topics. A quick and easy source of topics to get your students talking about human nature, interpersonal relationships, and North American society. There are eight different types of activities: talks, interviews, role plays, chain stories, discussions, and three group creativity activities.

Surveys for Conversation. High beginner and up. You assign a questionnaire for homework. The students answer the questions on the survey and come back to class prepared to say something on the topic. Topics include family, computers, love, health, the environment, crime, clothes, shopping, and 40 others.